Advance Praise for

While We Still Have Time

"Sheila was a tremendous help to us during the recount of the 2011 Wisconsin Supreme Court Election and later as we organized Wisconsin Citizens for Election Protection and Wisconsin Counts in our efforts to detect and prevent election fraud. Sheila, the world needs your experience and perspective. Thank you for not letting government oppression silence your voice. I hope that *While We Still Have Time* becomes widely read and that people follow your example and take action for justice."

Jim Mueller, J.D., a first amendment and election integrity activist in the Wisconsin battle for the 99%.

"After witnessing the blatant suppression of low income African-American voters in Columbus, Ohio in 2004, I became an activist and met Sheila, through some work we were doing together. Years have passed, with continued non-biased reports suggesting that election machines are unreliable, and can be subject to tampering without detection. Sheila's continual efforts through *While We Still Have Time* and The Center for Hand-Counted Paper Ballots, stand as beacons of hope and perseverance to those of us who care enough about this country to demand that elections are held fairly and reflect the will of the people."

Dorri Steinhoff, voting rights activist in the battleground state of Ohio

"Concerned about voter suppression, the war on women, Citizens United? Parks makes the connections to what mainstream media dangerously ignores—**the escalating crisis** that now seriously threatens our very democracy—election fraud—and why we must *occupy* vote counting. Parks offers her analyses, based on well researched and from-the-trenches information, pointing the way to honest elections. She shows us why we need Hand-Counted Paper Ballots, (HCPB) not electronic voting machines, now! This important book is a how-to on ensuring our votes do count—that all are counted—as cast, *While We Still Have Time.*"

Amy Bookbinder, Social Justice Educator/Activist, Northampton, MA

More Praise For
While We Still Have Time

"Regardless of what you believe about the security of electronic voting machines or where you stand on their widespread use, Sheila Parks' *While We Still Have Time,* is a must read. Sheila has been tirelessly researching and writing against voting machines since the 2000 presidential election; her book is a tour de force sure to be enlightening to anyone interested in the integrity of elections in the United States."

ANTHONY BUCCI, Ph.D. computer scientist

"Sheila Parks is one of America's greatest activists for women's rights and fair elections."

RICHARD CHARNIN, quantitative analyst with two masters' degrees in applied mathematics

"Dr. Sheila Parks' writings compel readers to re-evaluate how supposedly democratic processes are being implemented throughout the highways and byways of America. As one of the nation's foremost authorities on elections, she provides insightful arguments on why the only path to fair and transparent elections is hand-counted paper ballots with a secure chain of custody. Among my favorite chapters is "Down the Rabbit Hole with Democracy and Three Urgent Pleas," which skillfully reveals how government and societal practices are not in line with democratic values. Readers will value Parks' appreciation of diversity, depth of research and poignant thinking that shines through in all her writings."

JERROLL SANDERS, Author, *The Physics of Money: If You've Got My Dollar, I Don't* and race strategist.

"Sheila Parks is a brave, passionate and dedicated warrior, fighting on the front lines for women's rights, election integrity and human rights. I had the honor of meeting her when she visited Wisconsin to help us start to clean up our deeply flawed election system. She is one of our most sensitive spirits, a canary in the mine. Sheila is singing, and it is mandatory that we listen to her song. *While We Still Have Time* is an important and timely book."

SUE TRACE, Wisconsin Citizens for Election Protection

"It is to the everlasting shame of the so-called 'news media' that this election fraud, for which there is overwhelming evidence, has not been headline news. Every news journalist and every person who cares about this country should read *While We Still Have Time*—and then demand the common sense return to hand-counted paper ballots."

JANA NESTLERODE, J.D., Professor, Department of Criminal Justice, West Chester University

"While We Still Have Time is an absolute must read for anyone who is concerned about our corporate-controlled election system and the erosion of women's rights in America. Sheila Parks, a tireless advocate for truth, transparency, and justice, not only writes about it, she LIVES it!"

MARIANNE M. MOONHOUSE, election integrity activist, founding member of Wisconsin Citizens for Election Protection and Wisconsin Counts

"Sheila Parks is one of our great activists: dedicated, dogged and determined to protect our democracy at all costs. Her writings are essential to all of us."

HARVEY WASSERMAN, co-author of *Will the GOP Steal America's 2012 Election* and co-founder of the global grassroots No nukes/pro-Solartopia movement.

WHILE WE STILL HAVE TIME

The Perils Of Electronic Voting Machines And Democracy's Solution:

PUBLICLY OBSERVED, SECURE HAND-COUNTED PAPER BALLOTS (HCPB) ELECTIONS

Sheila Parks, Ed.D.

© Sheila Parks, Ed.D., MMXII

Cover and book design by Marc Alonso/Leap Year Press.

All copyrights reserved, with the exception of the following images from the Library of Congress Print and Photograph Collection, for which no known restrictions on publication exist: "The Fifteenth Amendment," lithograph by C. Rogan, c. 1871, Reproduction #: LC-DIG-pga-03453; "The first vote," Illus. from Harper's Weekly, v. 11, no. 568 (1867 November 16), p. 721, (title page), drawn by Alfred R. Waud (1828-1891) Call #: LOT 14013, no. 48 [P&P]; "Woman Suffrage, Leaving Jail," Harris & Ewing,(1918), Call #: LC-H261- 29910. "New York women voters in 1920" is used by permission from Brown Brothers, Sterling, PA.

"What Were They Fighting For?" © Natali Freed and Sheila Parks, 2012.

"Chapter VI: Hacking The Recalls: Why We Must Have Hand-Counted Paper Ballots and Citizen Exit Polls" © Grant Petty and Sheila Parks, 2011 and *"Chapter VIII: Hacking Our Elections with Big Money and Power,"* © Michael Collins and Sheila Parks, 2011 may be reproduced in whole or part with attribution of authorship and a link to the article.

Because pages on the web are frequently revised, updated, and occasionally removed and although every attempt was made to use the latest and most viable links to source documents, hyperlinked references to web pages may become outdated, or appear to be missing. Please note that the author does not offer any warranties, and is not responsible for any errors or omissions. The author assumes no liability for any damages resulting from the use of information in this work or for any infringement of the intellectual property rights of third parties that would result from the use of this information. This work is licensed under a Creative Commons Attribution-Noncommercial-NoDerivs Unported License (US/v3.0). Noncommercial uses are thus permitted without any further permission from the copyright owner. Individual chapters or portions thereof may be copied for educational purposes only.

For more information, see: http://creativecommons.org/licenses/by-nc-nd/3.0/.

For all voters in the United States of America and the whole world, who want the best possible assurance that their votes are counted as cast in secure, honest, accurate and transparent elections.

What Were They Fighting For?

What were they fighting for?
What were they fighting for?

What was she fighting for, Harriet Tubman?
What was she fighting for, Alice Paul?
What were they fighting for, Fanny Lou Hamer,
Martin, Malcolm, Goodman, Schwerner, Chaney?

Not for electronic theft of votes.
Not for corporate profits.

They starved, went to jail, fought back, were murdered.
They changed this world.
They used courage and voice.

Do we throw that away?
Florida 2000, Georgia 2002, Ohio 2004, Wisconsin 2011.

What were they fighting for? Equality.
What were they fighting for? Democracy.
What were they fighting for? A voice.

What are we fighting for? Transparency.
What are we fighting for, we the people? Our voice.
We want our votes to count.

I'll lend my hands.
WE MUST COUNT EACH VOTE BY HAND

© Natali Freed and Sheila Parks, 2012. This poem originally appeared as a song, written by Natali Freed and Sheila Parks. Sung by Natali Freed, <http://www.youtube.com/watch?v=vZ7Zoz7PI4g>. Updated 22 July, 2012.

Acknowledgements

On this journey of twelve years, I have met many wonderful people from all over the country who have enriched my work and my life. I am deeply thankful to call you colleague and many of you also friend.

To Kathleen Wynne and Sharona Merel, truth tellers still and from the beginning for hand-counted paper ballots now. To Deirde Doran, my very close friend over many years, for telling me I had to write this book. To Marie, who kept on telling me I had to publish this book. To Sandra, for listening, remembering, supporting me, and commenting wisely. To Arlene Montemarano, who tells me the most insightful and thoughtful things.

To Lucius Chiaraviglio, extraordinary web site master and a pleasure to work with. To Judy Lynch, who is always true and always helpful. To the National Writers Union in general and Barbara Beckwith and Barbara Mende in particular. The two Barbaras know everything, at least everything I want to know—and they share so generously. To Allison Francis, Anne Linn, Marie Hanson, Marjorie Minkin, Michelle Weiser, Mindy Fried, Sue Mundell, and another Sue for your finishing touches. To Marc Alonso, without whose many talents and skills this book would not have appeared in print.

To the wonderful Wisconsinites, whom I love and admire, still in the trenches and front lines and fighting back for honest elections.

To the Occupies, whom I love and admire, especially my friends from Occupy Boston.

Some chapters close with a thank-you list to people who grace my life by being in it and who gave special help, each in their own way.

To the many many people in my life, family and friends, for your lovingkindness, collaboration, corroboration, agreeing, disagreeing, fighting, making up, not making up—perhaps yet, having my back and your appreciation of my work and that of the Center for Hand-Counted Paper Ballots.

Utmost and deepest thanks to all the sisters and brothers everywhere, who are fighting against all injustice.

I am forever grateful to all of you.

Sheila XOXO
August, 2012

Contents

Introduction	19
Prologue	27

IT'S THE ELECTRONIC VOTING MACHINES, STUPID!

I. Hacking The Machines	37

ELECTION FRAUD—FLORIDA, GEORGIA, OHIO AND WISCONSIN STYLE

II. What Went Wrong in Ohio and Black Box Voting	45
III. Hand-Counted Paper Ballots Now	49
IV. Down the Rabbit Hole with Democracy and Three Urgent Pleas	57
V. Wisconsin: Democracy In Our Hands	71
VI. Hacking the Recalls: Why We Must Have Hand-Counted Paper Ballots and Citizen Exit Polls Grant Petty and Sheila Parks	81
VII. Center for Hand-Counted Paper Ballots Sends Letter to Recall Candidates Regarding Election Protection	89
VIII. Hacking Our Elections with Big Money and Power Michael Collins and Sheila Parks	93
IX. In Honor of the Anniversary of the Wisconsin Uprising, February 11, 2011—Wisconsin: the New Florida and Ohio?	97

WHAT DOES THE WAR ON WOMEN HAVE TO DO WITH THIS?

X. Crashing at the Intersection of Women's Rights and Voting Rights	111

XI. Hand-Counted Paper Ballots: Frequently Asked Questions 121

XII. On-Site Observations of the Hand-Counting of Paper Ballots and Recommendations for the General Election of 2008   131

XIII. Sort and Stack Elections in New Hampshire   143

XIV. The Following are Some Necessary Elements of Observed, Secure Hand-Counted Paper Ballots (HCPB) Elections   153

About the Author   159

Introduction

"Maybe you alone can't save the world, but it certainly won't be saved without you." *Fast Food for a Soul on the Run* by Harvey Arden.

I first began to work in this current wave of voting rights in 2000, in the midst of the presidential election crimes in Florida. Little did I know that, a dozen years later, I would still be very engaged in the same work, and that the situation would be even worse, much worse, now in 2012. Each voter must know that her or his vote counts and is counted as cast. This is one of the bedrocks of democracy.

Voters in the United States of America do not know for certain if their votes will be recorded and counted as they intended. In fact, there is ample evidence that the likelihood of votes not being counted accurately and as cast is high. For those who insist no such fraud exists, *While We Still Have Time* contains countless examples of election fraud and corruption, focused specifically on electronic voting machines.

The struggle for voting rights is long and fraught with peril. It includes many who fought courageously and people were murdered—lest we ever forget Birmingham Sunday and Addie Mae Collins, Cynthia Wesley, Carole Robertson and Denise McNair. The struggle for voting rights is not over; rather it takes another form, as the privatized electronic voting machine industry (a few corporations, some transnationals) tampers with our votes. This tampering with our votes was sanctioned by the Supreme Court of the United States in 2000, in Bush v. Gore. This book deals only with the fraud of the electronic voting machines; I am keenly aware of the new Jim Crow laws of voter ID. Many other people and groups are working against them.

Electronic voting machines have caused and exacerbated many of the crises we face today. Simply and starkly stated: elections using electronic voting machines are often rigged by deliberately not counting the votes as cast. As a result, men and women who have not legitimately received a majority of the vote are put into office.

Because of these dire times and for easy access for the reader, I have gathered all my published articles on voting rights over the years into this book. I chose not to update these articles because they discuss a specific time and place and give the reader a sense of events as they were happening. The original citation, including the publication date for each article, is on the last page of the chapter. In cases where I state the chapter has been updated, that is because I made a few minor editorial changes.

Several different groups and individuals have made Open Records Requests (ORR) to counties in Wisconsin to examine and hand-count the ballots from the June 5th recall of Governor Scott Walker in Wisconsin. That hand-counting is going on now while I write. Kathy Nickolaus, controversial clerk of Waukesha County, said that she was going to destroy the ballots before the activists examined and hand-counted them. Nickolaus has been stopped from doing that. You can read a detailed account at The Brad Blog of all the goings-on in Wisconsin about this public hand-counting.[1] While I wildly applaud the wonderful Wisconsonites for doing this, on the other hand, a secure chain of custody of the ballots no longer exists, if it ever did. So there is no way of really knowing what this hand-count can and will turn up. The counting of ballots must be done right the first time, to make sure there is no tampering with the ballots, ballot bags, or memory cards before, during or after the election. The implementation of publicly observed hand-counted paper ballots, with a secure chain of custody, and streamed over the internet and videotaped is the only way to guarantee an accurate and transparent count of the votes that people cast.

In 2010, J. Alex Halderman and Ariel J Feldman reported that they replaced the voting software of the Sequoia AVC Edge touch-screen DRE (Direct Recording Electronic) voting machine with Pac Man.[2] On August 14, 2012, Marianne M. Moonhouse published her updated painstaking and crucial research showing the Wisconsin municipalities that had in 2011-2012 swapped out one optical scan voting machine for two touch-screen EDGE machines at the invitation of Command Central.[3] See *"Chapter IX: In Honor of the Wisconsin Uprising"* middle page 100-102, for a more complete discussion of the swapping out.

In telephone conversations with Pamela Smith of Verified Voting on August 20, 2012, she told me that the only difference between EDGE I and EDGE II machines is that on the EDGE II a printer can be added. Smith sent me a link where there is much more information about EDGE.[4] In email communication on August 20, 2012, Moonhouse said that Command Central sells only Sequoia AVC EDGE touch-screens in Wisconsin, all or most of them EDGE II. They would have to be EDGE II because Wisconsin statutes require that all electronic voting machines have a voter-verified paper audit trail (VVPAT).[5]

In an email conversation with Halderman on August 20, 2012, in answer to my question about whether the Pac Man hack had been done on an Edge I or Edge II, he replied, "I believe the machine we worked on was an Edge I, although it sounds like the differences are slight. The TTBR [top-to bottom review by Debra Bowen in California in 2007] mentions that Edge I and Edge II use identical firmware (http://www.sos.ca.gov/voting-systems/oversight/ttbr/sequoia-doc-final.pdf, p.7). This implies that, from a software standpoint at least, the same kinds of attacks are very likely to be possible on both machines." The Moonhouse data shows a red swing. People in Wisconsin continue to work on this now, even as I write. I cannot help but wonder if Command Central offered these EDGE II machines swap out in order to rig the primaries, the Scott Walker recall on June 5, 2012, and the 2012 General Election.

As long as our votes are counted on electronic voting machines that not only have proprietary software but also can be rigged without leaving a trace of the hacking, we can never know for certain who won an election. Most of the votes in the United States of America are counted on such machines, except for the few jurisdictions across the country who count in the most democratic, accurate and transparent way possible: observed and with a secure chain of custody hand-counted paper ballots (HCPB) elections.

Adding to the insanity, no one really knows exactly who owns the corporations that own the electronic voting machines. Or who owns the people who own those corporations. Not only do they change hands and names fairly often, but also it is difficult, if not impossible, to access that information. I cannot find this information any longer, and this is also the case for the many voting rights activists who I have consulted.

However, on July 20, 2012, Bev Harris of Black Box Voting released a most remarkable press release about the current owners of some of the machines:

> "A press release today about the planned expansion of Unisyn into more USA locations renews attention on foreign ownership of corporations selling voting systems into the United States. **Unisyn is owned by a Malaysian gambling outfit.** [Emphasis mine.] Another major elections industry player, Canada's Dominion, purchased the massive Diebold Election Systems division (which it shares with ES&S); Dominion also owns Smartmatic, which handles electronic vote-counting in the Philippines and Belgium. Military voting is now handled in several states by Barcelona, Spain-owned Scytl. In January 2012, Scytl acquired the largest election results reporting firm, SOE Software.

> Accenture, now based in Dublin Ireland (formerly headquartered in tax-haven Bermuda), claims copyright over the massive electronic voter registration/voter history databases used in several states, including Pennsylvania, Tennessee, Colorado, Wisconsin and Arkansas. Accenture purchased its voter registration unit from Election.com, a Saudi-owned company based in the Cayman Islands..."⁶

Harris continued this stunning story on July 25:

> "In my story last week, I described the transnational nature of today's privatized electronic vote-counting vendors, leading with a ramped-up effort to install machines into several U.S. states by Unisyn, a firm owned by Malaysian gambling behemoth Berjaya subsidiary, International Lottery and Totalizator.
>
> What would Malaysian gambling corporations want with American elections, you might ask. Well, clearly they want the state of Florida. Another Malaysian gambling outfit, the Genting Group, owned by another set of billionaires, had its stock price questioned when it ran into a "legislative blockage" in Florida; undaunted, this firm has now teamed up with a former Rick Scott [ultra-right-wing Republican governor of Florida; see *"Chapter X: Crashing at the Intersection of Women's Rights and Voting Rights."*] spokesman to see if it can rewrite some of Florida's state constitution, while pushing some legislators to get new laws drafted.
>
> Las Vegas-style casinos in Miami, here we come.
>
> Read through the excerpts below and you'll see what I mean. **This Malaysian gambling corporation is throwing money at Republicans and Democrats alike, but at a ratio of 4:1 towards Republicans.** [Emphasis mine.] Politics is about big money...."⁷

I do not believe that the American people have become as right wing as the 2010 election of the ten ultra-right-wing governors would indicate or the July 2012 recall win by Scott Walker. (See again *"Chapter X"*) Is your state the next Wisconsin—with an ultra-right-wing governor razing to the ground everything in sight that progressive forces have built over the years?

Highlighting two (there are many more, e.g. LGBTQ rights, including marriage) of the most brazen, barefaced and shameful examples of what voting on electronic voting machines has brought us: the war on women and the war on our planet—by denying the climate crisis. (Again, *"Chapter X"*) Do you want to kiss Roe v. Wade goodbye? Do you want to kiss our beautiful planet Earth goodbye, by ignoring the climate crisis? Our future is ominous—as long as we vote on electronic voting machines. Ultra-right-wing governors, who deny our climate crisis, gained office in Florida, Wisconsin and Ohio in 2010. Other ultra-right-wing Republicans who deny the climate crisis, are the Koch Brothers and the Chamber of Commerce.

Read what Bill McKibben tells us about the ultra-right wing and our climate crisis:

> "Left to our own devices, citizens might decide to regulate carbon and stop short of the brink; according to a recent poll, nearly two-thirds of Americans would back an international agreement that cut carbon emissions 90 percent by 2050. But we aren't left to our own devices. The Koch brothers, for instance, have a combined wealth of $50 billion, meaning they trail only Bill Gates on the list of richest Americans. They've made most of their money in hydrocarbons, they know any system to regulate carbon would cut those profits, and they reportedly plan to lavish as much as $200 million on this year's elections. In 2009, for the first time, the U.S. Chamber of Commerce surpassed both the Republican and Democratic National Committees on political spending; the following year, more than 90 percent of the Chamber's cash went to GOP candidates, many of whom deny the existence of global warming. Not long ago, the Chamber even filed a brief with the EPA urging the agency not to regulate carbon – should the world's scientists turn out to be right and the planet heats up, the Chamber advised, 'populations can acclimatize to warmer climates via a range of behavioral, physiological and technological adaptations.' As radical goes, demanding that we change our physiology seems right up there…"[8]

While We Still Have Time is about a we the people solution, a democracy solution to the errors, fraud, hacking and shenanigans that come with all the electronic voting machines, both DRE's/touchscreens and optical scans—namely and specifically and exactly—***publicly observed, and with a secure chain of custody, hand-counted paper ballots (HCPB) elections.***

Read the facts as they are gathered here. Read what others have written. Pick a few things from this list that call to you and do them. Come up with your own ideas. Follow your heart about what actions to take.

Give this book to at least five people you know and urge them to do the same.

Give this book to at least five people you don't know and ask them to do the same.

Ask your local libraries to buy a copy.

If you can afford to do so, buy a copy for your library.

Take the struggle to the streets. Start weekly vigils and/or sit ins—in front of your local clerk's office, at the office of your Secretary of State, at the corporate offices of the electronic voting machines industry, and any other places you think relevant. Give out flyers, a new one each week, if possible. Include your own thoughts and feelings about being cheated of your hard earned vote.

Post blogs.

Write letters to the editor and mail them.

Write op eds and submit them.

Write papers and publish them.

Write books and have them published.

Talk to everyone and anyone you can. Tell them that the Netherlands and Ireland don't use their electronic voting machines any longer. And in June 2012, Ireland sold all of them as scrap.

Show films, especially *Hacking Democracy* and *Recount*, in your own home and also at larger venues.

Write a love letter to HBO thanking them for airing these films and ask them to do it again and many times.

Take the struggle to the courts. Find out who has standing in your state to file an injunction to impound the electronic voting machines, the ballots in their ballot bags or boxes and the memory cards immediately after the polls close in an election that: is highly contested, is very close, might have questionable results or be rigged. See *"Chapter V: Wisconsin: Democracy in Our Hands"* for more detailed information about this.

Look into your state Constitution (most are online) to see if ballots must be counted openly or if electronic voting machines are legally allowed to count our votes.[9] If ballots must be counted openly, speak with a lawyer about how to proceed.

Look at The Voting Rights Act of 1965, amended in 2006. SECTION 1 says, "This Act may be cited as the 'Fannie Lou Hamer, Rosa Parks, and Coretta Scott King Voting Rights Act Reauthorization and Amendments Act of 2006.' Then it says "SEC. 2 (a) Purpose—The purpose of this Act is to ensure that the right of all citizens to vote, including the right to register to vote and cast meaningful votes, is preserved and protected as guaranteed by the Constitution."[10] One of the definitions of "meaningful" is "having great validity."[11] How can our votes be meaningful and have great validity if they are not counted as cast? A lawsuit about this now would be very meaningful to do.

Join a group doing this work.

Start a new group.

Work independently.

Work with a good friend, or two or three.
Join an Occupy.
Do mic checks—ask an occupier what it means.
Do non-violent direct action.

WHAT TO DO TODAY AND EVERY DAY UNTIL THE ELECTION ON TUESDAY, NOVEMBER 6, 2012: Send daily emails and make daily telephone calls to the clerk(s) of your city, town and county and to your Secretary of State (contact info is often on line by state) demanding that no electronic voting machines be used in the 2012 General Election. Paper ballots must be used and counted by hand. For people with disabilities to vote on, preferably the states should use Vote-Pad. See *"Chapter XIV Requirements for Secure Elections"* page 154 in the middle. If Vote-Pad is not available, a machine might have to be used, alas, but to be used only by people with disabilities, no exceptions.

It is a time to RESIST, educate, agitate, activate, organize, litigate, write, sing, dance, laugh, scream, whisper, holler, weep, rage. And then get up the next day and start all over again, *While We Still Have Time*.

Because "Your silence will not protect you," as Audre Lord so astutely told us.[12]

Sheila Parks, ED.D.
August 2012

Endnotes

[1] Brad Friedman, "Exclusive: Infamous Waukesha, WI Election Clerk Threatens to 'Destroy' Historic Walker Recall Ballots Amid Statewide Public Hand Count Effort," Bradblog.org, 13 August, 2012 <http://www.bradblog.com/?p=9470>.

[2] J. Alex Halderman and Ariel J. Feldman, "PAC-MAN on the Sequoia AVC-Edge DRE voting machine," <https://jhalderm.com/pacman/>.

[3] Marianne M. Moonhouse, "Command Central Deals in Wisconsin 2011-2012," handcountedpaperballots.org, 21 August, 2012 <http://www.handcountedpaperballots.org/documents/Command_Central_Deals_in_Wisconsin_2011-2012.html>.

[4] "Source Code Review of the Sequoia Voting System" by Matt Blaze, et al. "This report was prepared at the University of California, Berkeley under contract to the California Secretary of State as part of a Top-to-Bottom review of electronic voting systems certified for use in the State of California." See especially pages 12-16 on EDGE, Section 2.1.4.

[5] Thanks to Ross Hein of the Government Accountability Board (GAB) of Wisconsin for supplying me with this precise information. Wisconsin Legislative Documents, "Requisites for approval of ballots, devices and equipment," states: "If the device consists of an electronic voting machine, it generates a complete, permanent paper record showing all votes cast by each elector, that is verifiable by the elector, by either visual or non-visual means as appropriate, before the elector leaves the voting area, and that enables a manual count or recount of each vote cast by the elector." <http://docs.legis.wi.gov/statutes/statutes/5/III/91> state statute § 5.91 (18). See also the Election Administration Manual for random audits, page 125, <http://gab.wi.gov/sites/default/files/publication/65/election_administration_manual_8_15_12_pdf_30088.pdf>.

[6] Bev Harris, "(Multinational) 7/12—Electronic Vote-Counting Increasingly By Global Private Vendors," Black Box Voting.org, 20 July, 2012 <http://www.bbvforums.org/forums/messages/8/82176.html>.

[7] Bev Harris, "(Fl) 7/12—Malaysia, Gambling, Elections, Part II," Black Box Voting.org, 25 July, 2012 <http://www.bbvforums.org/forums/messages/8/82180.html>.

[8] Bill McKibben, "Global Warming's Terrifying New Math," Rolling Stone, 19 July, 2012 <http://www.rollingstone.com/politics/news/global-warmings-terrifying-new-math-20120719>.

[9] Nancy Tobi, e-mail conversation, 08 January, 2012.

[10] The Voting Rights Act of 1965, <http://www.justice.gov/crt/about/vot/vra06.php>.

[11] Collins English Dictionary—Complete and Unabridged © HarperCollins Publishers 1991, 1994, 1998, 2000, 2003.

[12] Audre Lord, "The Transformation of Silence into Language and Action," Sister Outsider: Essays and Speeches (1984, 2007, The Crossing Press; Berkeley, Toronto).

Prologue

At the beginning, only white propertied men had the right to vote. After enormous struggles by many that extended over the course of two centuries—African American men, women, and Native Americans got the vote through Amendments XIV, XV, and XIX, the Indian Citizenship Act of 1924, the Civil Rights Act of 1964, and the Voting Rights Act of 1965, which was renewed and amended in 1970, 1975, 1982 and 2006. The new voter ID laws, aimed at suppression of the vote of people of color, low income people, students and elders, are in essence destroying some of these very hard won gains. Many groups and individuals are working to thwart these voter ID laws. This book deals with how we are all now also losing our votes because of the fraud of the electronic voting machines. *While We Still Have Time*, we must now stop using all electronic voting machines in our elections and instead now move to publicly observed, secure hand-counted paper ballots (HCPB) elections.

"The Fifteenth Amendment," lithograph by C. Rogan, c. 1871. Library of Congress Prints and Photographs Division, Washington, D.C. 20540 USA, Reproduction Number: LC-DIG-pga-03453. A print showing President Grant sitting at a large table, with group of men clustered around (identified below print), signing the 15th amendment granting that the right to vote cannot be denied on basis of race or color. Vignettes along sides and bottom show African Americans in military service, at school, on the farm, and voting.

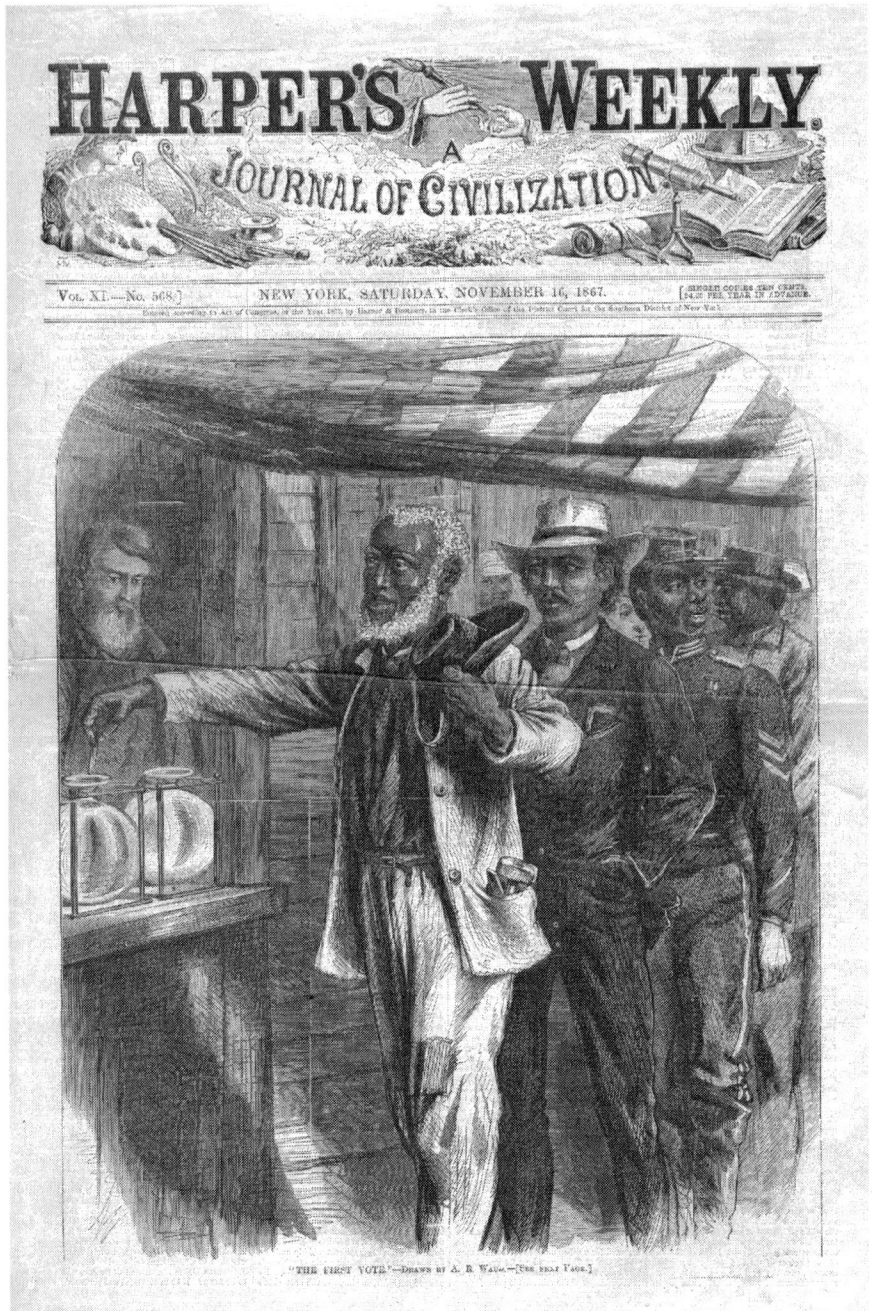

"The first vote" ; Illus. from: *Harper's Weekly*, v. 11, no. 568 (1867 November 16), p. 721 (title page); drawn by Alfred R. Waud (1828-1891) Library of Congress, Call Number: LOT 14013, no. 48 [P&P].

"Woman Suffrage, Leaving Jail." Harris & Ewing, photographer, 1918. Library of Congress Print and Photograph Collection, Call Number: LC-H261- 29910.

"New York women voters in 1920." Women voting for the first time, after Amendment XIX was ratified on August 18, 1920, certified on August 26, 1920 and became the law of the land. Permission granted from Brown Brothers, Sterling, PA.

It's the Electronic Voting Machines, Stupid!

I

Hacking The Machines

The Problem

A privatized electronic voting machine industry (corporations, some transnational) owns and therefore runs and controls our elections. Electronic voting machines can all be rigged: optical scan machines that use paper ballots that are then scanned electronically, and DRE's/touchscreen machines that don't use paper ballots. But take heed, anyone could hack these machines.

Some Noted Examples That Show Hacking Can Be Done To All Kinds Of Electronic Voting Machines

1. Research by Professor Edward W. Felten, Princeton University, showed that keys from hotel mini-bars, an office furniture store and those bought freely on the Internet, can open Diebold AccuVote-TS voting machines and leave no trace.[1]

2. The Vulnerability Assessment Team at the Argonne National Laboratory reported that an electronic voting machine model, Diebold AccuVote-TS, still expected to be used widely to count votes in the 2012 General Election, could be easily hacked—for about $10.50, by a student with an 8th grade science education using a remote control device. The Team states that voting results could be changed and no trace of the tampering[2] would be evident. VerifiedVoting.org has reported that over three million voters in Colorado, Indiana and Maryland will be using these machines.[3]

3. Alex Halderman (Univ of Michigan) and Ariel Feldman (Princeton), replaced the voting software of the Sequoia AVC Edge touch-screen DRE voting machine (used by almost 9 million voters in 2008) with Pac-Man.[4] They did this in three afternoons, without breaking any tamper-evident seals. "No word on plans to give Ms. Pac-Man suffrage."[5] says Kim Zetter of Wired.

4. The famous Hursti Hacks, by Finnish computer expert Harri Hursti—produced by Bev Harris and Black Box Voting—demonstrated (in multiple tests) that you can program a voting machine (Diebold Optical Scan) to do anything to votes, and with a little more work, you can make the fraud undetectable. Read the summary in the Wikipedia article[6] (has links to authoritative pages); then see "The Black Box Report," (July 4, 2005),[7] "Diebold TSx Evaluation," (May 11, 2006 and July 2, 2006),[8] and "Diebold TSx Evaluation Supplemental Report," (May 22, 2006 and July 2, 2006).[9]

5. "The federal agency responsible for inspecting voting equipment said Thursday [22 December, 2011] that a ballot scanner used in several key battleground states can freeze up without warning, fail to log errors and misread ballots." The Election Assistance Commission (EAC) [an independent agency of the US government, created by the Help America Vote Act—HAVA] put out a warning in December 2011 about ES&S DS200 IntElect optical scan electronic voting machines errors ***during voting*** [emphasis mine].[10] These machines were used in all or part of **Florida**, Illinois, Indiana, New York, **Ohio** and **Wisconsin** [emphasis mine]. Read more details on the "Politics Extra" blog at cincinnati.com[11] and on The Plain Dealer.[12] Shockingly, the machines will not be decertified. Said Brian Hancock of the EAC, "Our goal is not to decertify systems. We never want to be in a situation of putting counties in a position where they cannot run an election."

6. "Security experts have warned that electronic voting systems are decades away from being secure...,"and in a test of Washington DC's internet voting system for absentee ballots, Alex Halderman's team from the University of Michigan proved the insecurity of the system by hacking it to elect "drunken Futurama robot Bender" to be the head of the school board.[13]

7. At the RSA Conference 2012, David Jefferson, a computer scientist at Lawrence Livermore National Laboratories and chairperson of the election watchdog group Verified Voting, warned that "Internet voting systems are inherently insecure and should not be allowed in the upcoming general elections..."[14]

8. Clint Curtis, who used to be a Republican before this happened, was a computer programmer. He testified before Congress that Tom Feeney (Speaker of the House of Florida at the time) tried to pay him

to rig election vote counts by writing vote rigging software in South Florida.[15]

The Solution

Publicly observed, secure hand-counted paper ballots (HCPB) elections are the only way our votes must be counted. Votes must be hand-marked on paper ballots that are hand-counted twice at the polling place, right after the polls close, by opposing parties on the ballots, video taped and broadcast or streamed live over the internet, and results immediately posted in polling place windows for all to see. In *"Chapter XII: On-Site Observations of the Hand-Counting of Paper Ballots and Recommendations for the General Election Of 2008,"* Acton, ME could be and should be a model for the entire country (See p. 132).

This article originally appeared in Center for Hand-Counted Paper Ballots, 27 April, 2012 (http://www.handcountedpaperballots.org/documents/Hacking_the_Machines.html). Updated 13 July, 2012.

Endnotes

¹ Edward W. Felten, "Hotel Minibar Keys Open Diebold Voting Machines," Princeton University, 18 September, 2006 <https://freedom-to-tinker.com/blog/felten/hotel-minibar-keys-open-diebold-voting-machines/>.

² Brad Friedman, "Diebold voting machines can be hacked by remote control," 27 September, 2011 <http://www.salon.com/2011/09/27/votinghack>.

³ VerifiedVoting.org has reported that over three million voters in Colorado, Indiana and Maryland will be using these machines. <http://www.verifiedvoting.org/verifier/searched.php?ec=allall&state=AS&equipment_type%5B%5D=All+Types&vendor%5B%5D=All+Vendors&model%5B%5D=AccuVote-TS&vvpat=all&submit=Search&rowspp=50&topicText=&stateText=>.

⁴ J. Alex Halderman (University of Michigan) and Ariel J. Feldman (Princeton University), "PAC-MAN on the Sequoia AVC-Edge DRE voting machine," 09 August, 2010 <https://jhalderm.com/pacman/>.

⁵ Kim Zetter, "Touchscreen E-Voting Machine Reprogrammed to Play Pac-Man," Wired, 24 August, 2010 <http://www.wired.com/threatlevel/2010/08/pac-man/>.

⁶ Hursti Hack, Wikipedia, 18 May, 2012 <http://en.wikipedia.org/w/index.php?title=Hursti_Hack&oldid=493216669>.

⁷ Harri Hursti, "The Black Box Report, SECURITY ALERT: 04 July, 2005; Critical Security Issues with Diebold Optical Scan System Design," Black Box Voting, July 4, 2005 <http://www.blackboxvoting.org/BBVreport.pdf>.

⁸ Harri Hursti, "Diebold TSx Evaluation, SECURITY ALERT: 11 May, 2006; Critical Security Issues with Diebold TSx," Black Box Voting, Unredacted—Released 02 July, 2006, Black Box Voting <http://www.blackboxvoting.org/BBVreportIIunredacted.pdf>.

⁹ Harri Hursti, "Diebold TSx Evaluation, SECURITY ALERT: 22 May, 2006; Supplemental report, additional observations," Black Box Voting, Unredacted on 02 July, 2006, Black Box Voting <http://www.blackboxvoting.org/BBVreportII-supplement-unredacted.pdf>.

¹⁰ Gregory Korte, "Federal agency finds defects in ballot scanners," USA TODAY, 23 December, 2011 <http://www.usatoday.com/news/politics/story/2011-12-22/defective-voting-machines/52172034/1?mid=55>.

¹¹ "Cleveland voting machines miss votes, freeze up," Politics Extra blog (cincinnati.com) 23 December, 2011 <http://cincinnati.com/blogs/politics/2011/12/23/cleveland-voting-machines-miss-votes-freeze-up/>.

[12] Laura Johnston, "U.S. government investigation finds Cuyahoga County's election machines are flawed," The Plain Dealer, 23 December, 2011 <http://blog.cleveland.com/metro/2011/12/us_government_investigation_fi.html>.

[13] Iain Thomson, "Election hacked, drunken robot elected to school board," The Register, 01 March, 2012 <http://www.theregister.co.uk/2012/03/01/electronic_voting_hacked_bender/>.

[14] Jaikumar Vijayan, "Internet voting systems too insecure, researcher warns," Computerworld, 01 March, 2012 <http://www.computerworld.com/s/article/9224799/Internet_voting_systems_too_insecure_researcher_warns>.

[15] "Computer Programmer testifies that Tom Feeney (Speaker of the Houe of Florida at the time) tried to pay him to rig election vote counts." <http://www.youtube.com/watch?v=JEzY2tnwExs>.

*Election Fraud—
Florida, Georgia,
Ohio and
Wisconsin Style*

II

What Went Wrong in Ohio and Black Box Voting

In *Black Box Voting*[1] and *What Went Wrong in Ohio*,[2] Bev Harris and John Conyers (D-Michigan) present data that are chilling indictments of our election system. Harris discusses electronic voting machines and the fraud and error they have enabled in elections. Conyers highlights the disenfranchisement of African American, low-income, and Democratic communities through voter suppression by government power and campaign organizations; he also discusses problems associated with electronic voting machines.

A striking example from Harris: in March, 2002, Diebold Election Systems, one of the largest manufacturers of electronic voting machines, received a $54 million dollar contract to place these machines in the entire state of Georgia. Harris found "40,000 secret files on an unprotected" Internet site of Diebold.[3] One of the files was called "rob-georgia.zip." Rob-georgia.zip contained a patch for the Windows CE operating system that went unchecked and un-certified by any government official. With specific documentation, Harris states, "Talbot Iredale, senior vice president of research and development for Diebold…modified the Windows CE operating system used in Georgia." Harris concludes that a single man had unchecked access to modify the operating system on which the votes were counted—a major security breach. Her investigation showed that computer commands had been replaced on all 22,000 machines in Georgia "right before the election without anyone examining what the new commands actually do." In November, 2002, there were six Georgia contests in which Republicans won upset victories, the most notable being the race that Senator Max Cleland lost to conservative Republican Saxby Chambliss.

A year after the publication of her book, Harris and her organization, Black Box Voting, along with computer experts Harri Hursti and Hugh Thompson, publicly hacked Diebold optical scan electronic voting machines in Leon County, Florida in the presence of election supervisor Ion Sancho, thereby demonstrating the ease with which electronic voting machines can be rigged.

Conyers provides specifics about Ohio—e.g., that voters in some African American and Democratic communities had to wait in line ten hours to vote. Conyers argues that many of the problems in Ohio involved "intentional misconduct and illegal behavior," with Secretary of State Kenneth Blackwell playing a major role. One of many examples is Blackwell's restricting of provisional ballots, which disenfranchised "tens, if not hundreds, of thousands" of mostly minority and Democratic voters. Blackwell was cochair of the Bush-Cheney campaign in Ohio. Because of the numerous illegal activities, Conyers states that the Ohio electors "cannot be considered lawfully certified."

Conyers details the eye-opening story of Sherole Eaton, Deputy Director of Elections for Hocking County (a whistleblower, since fired). She reported that she saw Michael Barbian Jr., a representative of Triad Governmental Systems, Inc., modify the vote tabulator for the Hocking County computer prior to the Ohio recount announcement. Conyers adds that Psephos Corporation, a Triad affiliate, "supplied the notorious butterfly ballot used in Palm Beach County, Florida in the 2000 presidential election."

We must acknowledge and end the racism that plagues our country and voting system. The Voting Rights Act must be enforced and renewed by 2007. We must change to a system of hand-marked, hand-counted paper ballots (HCPB). Used in a number of democracies throughout the world and in some municipalities in the United States, HCPB are an excellent alternative to the current extensive use of electronic voting machines, which can be rigged regardless of how many mandated random audits are held, at whatever percent, on any machines—touch-screens or optical scans. Ballots must be counted correctly the first time. To audit HCPB, votes are counted by hand again, immediately after the first hand count. HCPB require safeguards, but these are more easily provided than making electronic voting machines that cannot be rigged.

If not now, when?

This article originally appeared in Tikkun, 01 January, 2006 (http://www.tikkun.org/nextgen/what-went-wrong-in-ohio-and-black-box-voting).

Endnotes

[1] Bev Harris, <u>Black Box Voting: Ballot Tampering in the 21st Century</u>, (Talion Press, 2004).

[2] Anita Miller, ed., <u>What Went Wrong in Ohio: The Conyers Report on the 2004 Presidential Election</u>, (Academy Chicago Publishers, 2005).

[3] Harris 88. "I'd found the crown jewels for Diebold Election Systems. What follows is the first detailed look—ever—into a secret voting system. What do you do when you find 40,000 secret files on an unprotected file transfer site on the Internet? Probably just look and go away. But what if you have pledged allegiance to the United States, and to the republic for which it stands? What if you knew that the devil went down to Georgia on November 5, 2002, and handed that state an election with six upsets, tossing triple-amputee war veteran Max Cleland out of the U.S. Senate in favor of a candidate who ran ads calling Cleland unpatriotic? Suppose you knew that in Georgia, the first Republican governor in 134 years had been elected despite trailing in every poll, and that African American candidates fared poorly even in their own districts?..."

III

Hand-Counted Paper Ballots Now

The right to vote, as well as the principle of "one person, one vote," are cornerstones of our democracy. The anti-slavery, women's suffrage, and civil rights movements as well as the expansion of voting to young people are all part of the history of electoral reform in this country. Equally fundamental is the assurance that each voter knows that her or his vote counts and is counted as intended. At this time in our history, many have lost confidence in our voting system.

The presidential elections of 2000 and 2004, and at least six contests in the mid-term elections of 2002, raised many questions about fraud and electronic voting machines.[1] The Help America Vote Act (HAVA) of 2002,[2] the U.S. Election Assistance Commission (EAC)[3] established by HAVA, and the Carter-Baker National Commission on Federal Election Reform[4] were all created after the 2000 election to improve the electoral process. All of these efforts, however, have been detrimental to the prevention and detection of election fraud and error due to their advocacy of the use of electronic voting machines. One election reform advocate, Bev Harris of Black Box Voting, provides a particularly vivid glimpse into the scope of the problems associated with electronic voting machines. She notes that, at a special Texas meeting of the Carter-Baker Commission, "I asked a member of the Panel why they [the Commission] had not asked a single question about how hacks can be done. He said it is not necessary to understand how the system can be compromised in order to protect it."[5]

The U.S. Government Accountability Office (GAO) in its nonpartisan September 2005 report on elections states in its conclusions: "Numerous recent studies and reports have highlighted problems with the security and reliability of electronic voting systems…the concerns they raise have the potential to affect election outcomes."[6]

Currently there is no government agency that regulates the voting machine industry in the United States. Roughly 80% of votes in the 2004 presidential election were cast and counted on machines manufactured by two private companies, Diebold and ES&S (Election Systems & Software, Inc.), both controlled by registered Republicans.[7] There are two principal types of machines now in use: (1) touch-screens (DRE—Direct Recording Electronic), on which for many no audit or recount is possible because they have no paper trail and (2) optical scans, which use paper ballots for the vote but are counted by central tabulators or at the precinct level (both particularly susceptible to fraud).

Although several bills currently pending in the U.S. House and Senate, introduced by both Republicans and Democrats, propose changes to electronic voting machines,[8] as do HAVA, the EAC and the Carter-Baker Commission, none consider hand-marked, hand-counted paper ballots (HCPB) as a solution. Most of the proposed legislation advocates for what is variously called a voter verified paper audit trail (VVPAT), a voter verified paper trail (VVPT) or a voter verified paper ballot (VVPB). A discussion of the nuances between and among these systems is beyond the scope of this article, but all share a potential weakness—namely, there is no way to prevent hacking of electronic voting machines later in the process, whether or not a voter receives a record of how she or he voted and/or whether there is a paper trail in the machine. Mandated random audits of the vote raise the question of whether the audit will really be random and bring back flashes of Florida in 2000 and a long drawn out struggle. Will the Supreme Court again put a non-elected person in office as president of the United States?

Although much has been published on the Internet, the mainstream media have mostly chosen to ignore or dismiss the questions of fraud and error raised in relation to electronic voting machines. Notable exceptions are discussions by Keith Olbermann on MSNBC's "Countdown" and Mark Crispin Miller's article "None Dare Call It Stolen" in *Harper's Magazine*,[9] in which he strongly suggests that the presidential election of 2004 was rigged, much of it by electronic voting machines.

HCPB are an alternative to the current widespread and increasing use of electronic voting machines. An HCPB system of voting has the following major advantages over electronic voting machines:

1. Counting of ballots is publicly done, observed and filmed by everyday citizens who are registered voters in the precinct where the counting takes place.

2. Security safeguards are much more easily built in to protect against tampering.

3. The cost is far less.

There have been two recent efforts to promote an HCPB system in the

United States, and a third will take place at some later time. In 2004, voting rights activists Sharona Merel, Karen Renick, Ellen Theisen, and Kathleen Wynne proposed federal legislation for federal offices.[10] In 2005, four voting rights activists (this writer and three members of CASE Ohio — John Burik, Phil Fry, and Dorri Steinhoff) began work on a protocol for HCPB. Some of this work, in modified form, has been incorporated here into the specifications for HCPB. Voting rights activist Joanne Karasak plans to promote a state constitutional amendment for HCPB in Ohio.[11] There are 18 states where such constitutional amendments are possible.[12]

The key elements of an HCPB system are as follows:

1. Electronic voting machines are not involved in this process in any way whatsoever.

2. Each voter hand marks a sturdy paper ballot with a black felt pen provided at the precinct.

3. The counting process happens at each precinct immediately after the polls close.

4. Each ballot is hand-counted by registered voters from that precinct in full view of other registered voters from that precinct.

5. The counting process is recorded on video and carefully archived for easy future reference.

6. Results are posted at each precinct, immediately after the counting.

7. A chain of custody of the ballots and ballot boxes is specified.

8. Ballot boxes are observed and a video record is created as boxes are opened and closed and move from place to place.

Three categories of registered voters are included in this process: the official counters, the official observers of the counters, and the public watchers of the counters and observers. The hand-marked, paper ballots are hand-counted in full view of the public in each precinct by a specified number of registered voters in that precinct—e.g., four, six or eight voters. Half of the counters will consist of one person from each party on the ballot, chosen by the party itself; the other half of the counters will consist of registered voters, chosen by lottery. The hand-counting is observed by the same number of registered voters (e.g., four, six or eight), and chosen in the same way as the counters. Counting is recorded by a video projection unit; a process will be set up to determine how the videotaping unit will be selected. The videotaping will be broadcast over closed-circuit TV and streamed over the Internet while the counting is happening. Any participants may also videotape and/or take photographs at any time.

Each polling place must be arranged so that registered voters from those precincts (in addition to the above mentioned official observers) can easily watch the vote counting. These watchers are not to be confused with the observers of the counters. Watchers will include two registered voters from each party on the ballot, chosen by the party, and eight registered voters chosen by lottery. The polling place must be large enough to accommodate these numbers.

Even with all these safeguards in place, the chance for fraud still exists. Therefore, immediately after the first count, there will be a 100% hand-counted audit of the vote, carried out in the same way as the first hand count, but in the audit, the observers will be the counters and the counters will be the observers.

Ballot boxes must be clearly marked and visible in plain view. Ballot boxes will be sealed and locked whenever they contain ballots and are not being actively used. Ballot boxes are secured from the beginning of voting until the end of counting by a chain of custody procedure. Ballot boxes never leave the polling place until after the vote is counted, audited and certified. Each time ballot boxes move from the physical control of or visual contact from one person to another, a duplicate record signed by all counters and observers must be made relinquishing and gaining control. There will be a documentation process wherein each ballot box will have a record of its handling from the beginning of the day to the end of counting. Such a process exists currently and has been clearly detailed as a protocol titled "Ballot and Ballot Box Transportation" and "Ballot Storage" on the web site of computer science expert Professor Douglas W. Jones.[13]

The call to action is HCPB now.[14] Canada already uses an HCPB system for its federal races. Various states and municipalities already have protocols for HCPB. These could easily be adapted from one jurisdiction to another. Consult *Chapters XI, XII, XIII* and *XIV* in the section *"Hand-Counted Paper Ballots 101."* Elections are governed by state rather than federal statutes (HAVA notwithstanding). According to electionline.org, a website that provides an ongoing analysis of election reform, "Each state strikes a unique balance in allocating responsibility for elections between state and local governments. A survey of all 50 states reveals a wide spectrum of power-sharing arrangements."[15] There is a "Snapshot of the States" on pp. 11-14 of the Election Reform Briefing.[16] When you begin this work, call your local Secretary of State and get the exact rules for your state.

It is time to make electronic voting machines a NIMBY (not in my back yard and not in anyone else's back yard either) issue. To begin a movement for HCPB, ordinary citizens, registered voters, must begin organizing door-to-door with their neighbors to petition their local election officers and demand HCPB in their city or town. Although organizing could also proceed on a state level, going municipality by municipality is a good way to start, depending on your state's laws.

This article originally appeared in the April 2006 issue of Tikkun, as "Hand-Counted Paper Ballots in 2008" (http://www.tikkun.org/article.php?story=20090327095732653). This updated version appeared in Election Fraud News (http://electionfraudnews.com/archive/HCPB/Parks.htm).

Endnotes

[1] Sheila Parks, "What Went Wrong in Ohio and Black Box Voting," Tikun, 01 January, 2006 <http://www.tikkun.org/nextgen/what-went-wrong-in-ohio-and-black-box-voting>.

[2] 42 U.S.C. § 15301 *et seq.*

[3] 42 U.S.C. §§ 15321-15330.

[4] Commission on Federal Election Reform, 19 September, 2005 <http://www.american.edu/ia/cfer/>.

[5] "We knew they'd miss this boat," BlackBoxVoting.org/bbvforums, 19 September, 2005 <http://www.bbvforums.org/cgi-bin/forums/board-auth.cgi?file=/1954/10345.html>. Scroll down to "3. Voting Technology," which is in red and is the last comment in this section.

[6] "Federal Efforts to Improve Security and Reliability of Electronic Voting Systems Are Under Way, But Key Activities Need to be Completed," United States Government Accountability Office, September 2005 <http://www.gao.gov/new.items/d05956.pdf>.

[7] Lynn Landes, "Voting Systems Orgs And Companies," 2005 <http://ecotalk.org/VotingMachineCompanies.htm>.

[8] See e.g., "Voter Confidence and Increased Accessibility Act, H.R. 550," 109th Cong. (2005).

[9] M.C. Miller, "None dare call it stolen: Ohio, the election, and America's servile press," Harper's Magazine, August, 2005. See also his even stronger book, M.C. Miller, Fooled Again. (New York: Basic Books, 2005).

[10] Federal Paper Ballot Emergency Act of 2004 (proposed legislation) Votersunite.org 2004 <http://www.votersunite.org/takeaction/now-legislation-print.htm>.

[11] Personal communication, April, 2005.

[12] Initiative & Referendum Institute at the University of Southern California, "Helpful Handouts," <http://www.iandrinstitute.org/Quick%20Fact-Handouts.htm>.

[13] The University Of Iowa Department of Computer Science, Voting and Elections web pages /"Voting on Paper Ballots" specifically, see the sections "Ballot and Ballot Box Transportation" and "Ballot Storage" (the last two on the following link) <http://www.cs.uiowa.edu/~jones/voting/paper.html>.

[14] Although it is too late to change to HCPB for the 2006 elections, a beginning must be made now for the 2008 elections. The hacking of the electronic voting machines by Harri Hursti, working with Black Box Voting; the problems that occurred with electronic voting machines in many states in the recent 2006 primaries; the law suits

against the electronic voting machine companies; the paper by Ed Felton *et al* from Princeton University in Sept. 2006; the report of the Brennan Center Task Force of NYU, on June 27, 2006; the outstanding article by Robert F. Kennedy, Jr. in *Rolling Stone* (Issue 1002, June 15, 2006); articles in *The New York Times*, *The Washington Post* and other mainstream newspapers; and Lou Dobbs on CNN have hopefully made a more receptive climate for such change if not now on November 7, 2006, certainly by 2008. Two important questions must be addressed. First, should HCPB be initiated all at once for the entire ballot or only for federal races (i.e., for the president/vice president; U.S. Senator; U.S. Representative)? A dilemma is raised by this question. On the one hand, with a long or complicated ballot, HCPB might be difficult to initiate *in toto*. Moreover, because taking smaller, incremental steps might be more acceptable to doubters, starting with federal races first, and then adding local races, might be a better way to proceed. On the other hand, beginning only with HCPB in federal races implies falsely that local races are not as important and, therefore, electronic voting machines can be used for local contests. A second question that must be asked is as follows: should HCPB be used for all contests or only for federal races?

[15] "Election Reform Briefing, September 2002, Working Together? State and Local Election Coordination," Electionline.org <http://www.pewtrusts.org/uploadedFiles/Working_Together.pdf>.

[16] "Election Reform Briefing" 11-14

IV

Down The Rabbit Hole With Democracy And Three Urgent Pleas

Democracy. Who used to have it in the USA, and who has it now? People with white skin privilege? People who were born male? People with piles of money, much of it stolen from other people's labor?

I often hear European Americans from all walks of life talking about democracy in the USA—how they want to reclaim it, like in the good old days—and I wonder about how differently from one another we experience this country. This is not our land; not my land nor your land. When European Americans arrived over 500 years ago, we murdered with bullets and small pox blankets—that we intentionally gave to them—the Indigenous people who had lived in balance here for thousands of years. Then we enslaved people of African descent to build the country's wealth, and kept women—who did not even get the vote until 1920—second class citizens and the property of men for even longer.

The United States government is not a shining light. We never have been, and we are not now. While it was never really good for too many people, what has changed here in the USA is that it has gotten worse, not better. Our own elections system is now a corporate-controlled charade, with big money pulling all the strings and using electronic voting machines to rig the elections. And as we pretend to spread "democracy" all over the world, what we are really spreading is a devastating complex of illegal, immoral wars, both here and abroad.

When our children and grandchildren ask me what I am doing in this crucial time to stop our government from murdering people at home and abroad, I want to be able to tell them that I am doing *everything I possibly can* to get democracy in this country *for all the people, for the first time ever,* and to end these brutal behaviors everywhere. Don't you?

Clicking and sending e-mail and online petitions against the myriad, devastating problems facing us now is fine as far as it goes. But half-measures avail us nothing. Pleading with the people who make and then carry out the murderous policies of the USA government is time wasting at best and ridiculous at worst. Although, we did get to keep some funding for Planned Parenthood, through an Amazonian effort.

We here in the USA need to follow and emulate the examples of the people in Tunisia, Egypt and Wisconsin. The people of Tunisia and Egypt non-violently resisted immoral and murderous governments, and they won. Tunisia has ruled that there must be equal numbers of women and men who are candidates in their upcoming July election.[1] Egypt is still in process and we look especially to what they do about women's rights.[2] Juan Cole and Shahin Cole have written a wonderful article: "An Arab Spring for Women."[3]

During the Mubarak reign of terror, Egypt used to count its ballots by hand, a close Egyptian friend has told me. Everyone knew those elections were rigged, she added. That means that when we suggest to the Egyptian people that they continue to hand-count their votes now, but with very different protocols, to safeguard the counting and election, we have a different job ahead of us from demanding that here in the USA we hand-count all the ballots.

The Organization for Security Cooperation in Europe, OSCE, wrote recently about helping Tunisia with "free and fair elections." Part of OSCE's mandate is fair elections. The OSCE web site has an unbelievable final report summary on the 2004 USA presidential election[4] that they were invited to observe; OSCE thought the election was fine. Given that conclusion, the assistance of OSCE for Tunisia might not be so helpful.

Wisconsin must continue the magnificent uprising it has begun against the corrupt politicians who are attacking unions, the middle class, and women's rights.

However, Wisconsinites, please take heed: doing recalls on hackable electronic voting machines, the same machines that put in office those you are trying now to recall, is not such a good strategy (see more below). I have been involved in the current wave of Voting Rights since the 2000 presidential election in Florida. I have observed two hand-counted paper ballots (HCPB) recounts in real time. I have also observed several HCPB elections in real time, and have written about these elections and other voting rights issues. These papers can be found on the web site of the non-profit organization I founded, Center for Hand-Counted Paper Ballots.[5] The site has much information about the hacking of the machines by researchers and computer experts, documents in favor of hand-counted paper ballots elections, and other related topics.

First Urgent Plea: We here in the USA must non-violently resist our immoral and murderous government: with direct action, civil disobedience, civil resistance.

Immoral wars abroad against Iraq, Afghanistan, Pakistan, Libya, and supporting Israel in its wars against Gaza.

Immoral war at home against women and our bodies. Some still think that other issues need all our attention now and these are "only" women's rights that we can attend to after all the other important rights are fixed. The savage attempted and successful attacks on women's bodies by governors and both national and local legislatures feel like rabid dogs relentlessly biting us. Do you read *Jezebel, Feministing, Angry Black Woman, Feministe' Ms.*?

Immoral war at home against people of color. More African Americans are in prison now in the USA than there were in South Africa during all of Apartheid. See Michelle Alexander, *The New Jim Crow: Mass Incarceration in the Age of Colorblindness*.[6] Ask any of these inmates languishing in our vast prison complex—mostly on non-violent drug charges—how democracy works for them. Have you read Charles Ogletree's, *The Presumption of Guilt: The Arrest of Henry Louis Gates, Jr. and Race, Class and Crime in America*? Ogletree includes stories of one hundred African American men and shows how "race trumps class".[7] Do you know that our prisons are now increasingly privatized, and that Dick Cheney is one of those making so much money on them?

Immoral war against Native Americans. Trapped on reservations plagued with poverty, alcoholism, drug abuse and record levels of suicide; Leonard Peltier has been languishing in prison since 1977, with a release date of perhaps 2040. "….how the Bill of Rights failed….Choke on your blue white and scarlet hypocrisy…." sings Buffy Sainte-Marie in *My Country 'Tis Of Thy People You're Dying*.[8]

Immoral nuclear power plants. Building more of them is still on Obama's agenda, even after Fukushima, now called worse then Chernobyl, despite the corporate media white-out of the radiation now contaminating the water, soil and air across the globe. Do you know that Exelon, major nuclear power plant operator, was one of the highest contributors to Obama, both in Illinois when he was Senator and when he ran for the White House? Do you know that Representative Edward Markey, Democrat from Massachusetts, a high ranking and supposedly good player about nuclear power plants, has introduced legislation[9] asking for new, better and safer nuclear power plants, rather than no more nukes, no more weapons of mass destruction?

Immoral war against the climate and the planet itself. As the climate crisis reaches its tipping point, the corporate government hides its ostrich head in the sand while cutting back on investment in sustainable, renewable energy, like sun and wind power.

Immoral war against LGBTQ people. Many suicides by LGBTQ youth and attacks and murders of LGBTQ people shine a bright light on the homophobia and heterosexism of our society. LGBTQ people still cannot marry in most states, even though President Obama has said he is for gay marriage and the armed forces saga continues, even though there is now a temporary ban on enforcing "don't ask, don't tell." There has never been enough money spent for AIDS research.

Immoral war against whistleblower Bradley Manning.[10] After months of torture at Quantico, he is finally being moved to Leavenworth, a medium security prison. The army says the move had nothing to do with public pressure.[11] Clicking and sending helped here.

Immoral war against our food supply with genetically modified organisms (GMO's) that are not even labeled. We have a right to know exactly what is in the food we eat. GMO's have known health risks, "including infertility, immune problems, accelerated aging, faulty insulin regulation, and changes in major organs and the gastrointestinal system."[12] GMO's are also dangerous to the environment. "Up to 90% of U.S. soybeans, corn, cotton, canola, and sugar beets are now genetically engineered and routinely inserted into human and animal foods with no labels or safety testing." See Organic Consumers Association and Millions Against Monsanto[13] and Institute for Responsible Technology GMO Basics.[14] And the latest crime against us: USDA now moves to let Monsanto do its own studies.[15] Eat organic.

Immoral wars against most of its people. Now the government is at war with most of its people in all ways, except the ultra rich.

If I have left out your favorite screams and/or weeps, I apologize in advance. These are mine; I could have gone on and on.

Second Urgent Plea: Please pay attention to those of us who educate, write, investigate, litigate, legislate and talk about the rigging of our elections by all electronic voting machines.

The putsch with electronic voting machines is a more devious way of murdering us. There are two major kinds of electronic voting machines: Direct Recording Electronic (DRE's/Touchscreens) and optical scan (op scans or opti scans) voting machines. My friend and colleague, Lucius Chiaraviglio, has most aptly renamed then "op scams." All computer systems can be manipulated without detection, and so amount to an illegal, hidden ballot count. Do you know that our elections are owned and operated by a privatized voting machine industry?

The mess in Wisconsin now for the Supreme Court election has once again put vote counting and our elections in the spotlight. My friend and colleague, Victoria Collier, has published a significant paper on the subject at www.votescam.org.[16]

Rigging, tinkering with or manipulating elections is a bi-partisan equal opportunity. Republicans and Democrats are involved:

Republicans:

- Florida, 2000. Kathleen Harris, Secretary of State, with strong ties to the Republican party. See The Brooks Brothers Riot, where paid Republican operatives, pretending to be ordinary voters, tried to stop the recount in Florida.[17]

- Florida, 2000. See David Barstow and Don Van Nata, Jr., *How Bush Took Florida: Mining the Overseas Absentee Vote.*[18]

- Georgia, 2002. Paraplegic liberal and popular Democratic Senator Max Cleland loses in an "upset victory" to conservative Republican Saxby Chambliss, as reported by Bev Harris, noting that there were six Georgia contests in which Republicans "won upset victories".[19]

- Ohio, 2004. Kenneth Blackwell, Secretary of State, with strong ties to the Republican Party, promises to deliver Ohio to Bush. In *What Went Wrong in Ohio* John Conyers argues that many of the problems in Ohio involved Blackwell taking a major role in "intentional misconduct and illegal behavior."[20]

- Wisconsin, 2011. The election for a seat on the Wisconsin Supreme Court was won by Republican incumbent Justice David Prosser by 7,316 votes. The difference is small enough between Prosser and challenger JoAnne Kloppenburg, to allow a recount. On April 19, 2011, the Independent candidate, JoAnne Kloppenburg who lost, asked for a statewide recount. She asked for a hand-count of ballots only in some districts, to be determined by working with the Government Accountability Board (G.A.B.) Brad Blog has noted that recount protocol in Wisconsin[21] allows only for a recount by the same machines that were used in the election, unless there is a court order for a hand-counted recount. Because some of the jurisdictions would have required erasing the memory cards from the election in order to make room for the data from the recount, Dane County Circuit Judge Richard Niess ordered a hand-recount in 31 counties, including another 14 municipalities in Milwaukee County and 34 municipalities in Waukesha County.[22] Both Prosser and Kloppenburg went along with this. The JSOnline, *Milwaukee Wisconsin Journal Sentinel* has an interesting description of what the recount will look like at <http://www.jsonline.com/news/statepolitics/120518594.html>. *The Voting News* has more information about the Wisconsin Recount.[23] Recount begins April 27, 9 AM.

A huge standing ovation to Kloppenburg for her courage, for standing strong and for her refusal to cede and cave a la Gore, Kerry, and Coakley in Massachusetts. And some possible perils: By now there is no secure chain of custody of the ballots and ballot boxes (if there ever was one) and that will present very serious problems for an honest recount. Not only must she do a statewide recount, but also she must use the same methods for the recount across the whole state (which is not going to happen, alas), or she could perhaps be in the same fix as Al Gore was in Florida, 2000. See Bush, et al. vs. Gore, *et al.*[24] and Paul Lehto, J.D. on Bush v. Gore.[25] And the entire recount must be done by hand, (which both sides have already agreed not to do, another alas), or else the ballots will be passed through the same op scan machines that were used the first time and could have been rigged then, and could be rigged in the recount. Then there are the DRE's that cannot be recounted, just the same results printed again from the same machines. I hope she will have her team take pictures of each and every ballot, whether recounted by hand or op scans. Of course there are no ballots for the DRE's, so there can be no pictures. You can send an e-mail to the Kloppenburg Campaign at Campaign@Kloppenburgforjustice.com.

Democrats:
- Why did Al Gore not protest the Supreme Court appointment of George W. Bush as the next president? As he rolled over without a fight, he stated, "…And tonight, for the sake of our unity of the people and the strength of our democracy, I offer my concession…."[26] What unity? What democracy? With an appointment to the presidency in a political vote by the Supreme Court of the United States? See also Jeffrey Toobin, *The Nine: Inside the Secret World of the Supreme Court.*[27]
- Why did Obama, in his acceptance speech in Chicago, proudly talk about the elder woman, a former slave of African descent, who put her finger out and touched the screen for his name?[28] He knew the

- dangers thereof; he has been contacted by scores of voting rights activists, as has Clinton, *et al.* "….And this year, in this election, she touched her finger to a screen, and cast her vote, because after one hundred and six years in America, through the best of times and the darkest of hours, she knows how America can change…."

- Was Obama's statement a prelude to Hillary Clinton asking India to help newly born Egypt with its elections?[29] India uses paperless Electronic Voting Machines (EVMs), the worst possible technology, though an Election Commission is now calling for a "paper trail of votes cast."[30]

Third Urgent Plea: We need publicly observed, secure hand-counted paper ballots (HCPB) elections now.

That each of our votes is counted as cast is the bedrock of democracy. Voting rights are the rights that all our other rights stand on. We need more organizations to take a stand for totally transparent, secure hand-counted paper ballots (HCPB) elections, where we are not asked to "trust" the results.

At The Center For Hand-Counted Paper Ballots,[31] you can learn how several jurisdictions in the United States hand-count their votes. (Also, see "*Chapter XII: On-Site Observations of the Hand-Counting of Paper Ballots and Recommendations for the General Election Of 2008.*") These are observations I made in real time of hand-counted paper ballots (HCPB) elections. Scroll especially down to Acton, Maine. This could be a model for the whole country.

Vote Rescue[32] in Texas, founded by Vickie Karp and Karen Renick, is the only other organization dedicated solely to hand-counted paper ballots (HCPB) elections, with no fall back position or compromise they are willing to make for political motives.

The following are some necessary elements of secure hand-counted paper ballots (HCPB) elections:

- Hand-counting is done for all races and initiatives, not only federal.

- The hand-counting process will be easily understood by a third grade student.

- No precinct is larger than 1000 registered voters.

- Hand-counting done at each precinct, immediately after polls close.

- Poll books of voters checking in and poll books of voters checking out must exactly match.

- Get rid of all e-poll books.

- The number of ballots counted must exactly match the number of ballots distributed.

- The number of ballots printed must match the number of ballots distributed, voted, and not voted

- No absentee ballots will be allowed, except for people in dire need and these ballots must be accounted for, managed, and counted in a procedure that is yet to be written.

- Hand-counting is done by teams of opposing parties on the ballot, chosen by the parties themselves.

- Other smaller parties can also be on hand-counting teams, in addition to those opposing parties on the ballots—e.g. Greens.

- Hand-counting is done by new people coming in to count, not those who have been working at the polls all day.

- Hand-counters are paid a very good hourly rate. This not only pays for one of the most important jobs in a democracy, but also keeps the money in the community and is far less expensive than buying, maintaining, upgrading and storing electronic voting machines.

- Hand-counting is done in full view of the public.

- Hand-counting is done twice and the results must match.

- Hand-counting is videotaped by any member of the public who wants to do so, while it is being done and also by official videographers, one from each opposing parties on the ballot.

- Hand-counting results are posted at the precinct, in the windows, after the counting so that all can see easily after polls close.

- No electronic voting machines, computers, or modems of any kind are allowed in any part of the hand-count.

- The Vote-PAD provides a means for people with disabilities to mark a ballot without requiring the use of electronic voting machines. It is essential to the enfranchisement of people with disabilities, that they do not use electronic ballot marking devices (such as the AutoMARK) which are frequently marketed to assist people with disabilities. The AutoMark can steal votes just like any other electronic voting machine. In personal correspondence with Ellen Theisen, on May 1 and 2, 2011, Theisen said, "Vote-PAD is no longer available, except in the twenty-two Wisconsin municipalities that purchased it and are currently using it....It provides the same paper ballot for people with disabilities as the ballot for others, and then all [ballots] are hand-counted together." (See Vote-PAD rocks the disabled vote.)[33]

- The hand-count, which has been done twice, will be the official count of the election from each precinct.

- This section on chain of custody and security of the ballots and ballot boxes is a work in progress.

- *Ballot and Ballot Box Transportation & Ballot Storage* (last two sections) by Doug Jones[34] gives many details of how to secure the ballots and their boxes

- See more details of security of ballots and their boxes by Sheila Parks.[35] Scroll down to third paragraph from the end

- Ballot boxes will be of clear plastic with a lock on each of the four corners. These boxes will be kept in full view of the election officials and the public at all times, from before the official opening time of the polls until the official election results are posted in the windows of each precinct.

- The locks on the ballot boxes will have two keys only, that is, one key will open two of the locks and another key will open the other two locks.

- There will be only one key for each of the two keys above. There will be no copies of keys.

- A Republican election official will hold one key and a Democrat election official will hold the other key.

- The ballot boxes will not be opened until all votes have been cast and the polls are closed.

- The ballot boxes will be opened in full view of the public.

- After the votes are hand-counted, the ballots will be placed in steel containers with seals on them.

- A secure chain of custody for the ballots and ballot boxes must be written from the precinct level to where they will be stored.

Other Major Problems with our Election System

Furthermore, there are several problems with our voting process, not only that our votes are not counted as cast, because of the fraud and error associated with all electronic voting machines, but also, that even if these problems were all fixed, the electronic voting machines would continue to rig our elections. And even if we had publicly observed, secure hand-counted paper ballots (HCPB) elections, the problems listed below would still exist. Our voting system is a hydra-headed weapon of mass destruction:

- Suppression of the votes of students, low income people, African Americans, Latinas, elders.

- A white-out of the news from any candidates the corporate media does not want to be elected.

- A white-out of the news from the corporate media of any of the fraud and rigging that voting rights activists have been pointing out and writing about at least since Florida 2000 presidential race.

- Corrupt election officials who run our elections and have strong past and present ties to the right wing of the Republican Party.

- Corrupt and/or incompetent voting election officials from both Democratic and Republican parties, and most likely all other parties too.

- Endless corporate money into coffers of candidates.

- Requiring of voter ID photos, which are issued only by the state, e.g., Department of Motor Vehicles, in order to vote.

- Absentee ballots, with both parties increasingly calling for more.

- Mail-in voting

- The election of two senators from each state means, e.g., that the voters in North Dakota and Vermont have an influence that is hugely disproportionate to voters in California.

Resisting in Real Time

April 15, 2011, as the House passed the brutal 2012 Budget Resolution,[36] "….During the debate, nine protesters were removed from the House gallery. Sitting in various parts of the visitors' chambers, the protesters, mostly young men and women, would stand up one-by-one and ad lib lyrics to "The Star Spangled Banner" and "We Shall Overcome…"

April 21, 2011 at a breakfast with Obama, some of his donors sang a song to him about Bradley Manning, before they were ushered out.[37]

April 2011. The arrest of young, pregnant women and young mothers, students at Catherine Ferguson School in Detroit, Michigan. The students and one teacher were arrested for protesting the closing of their school, as they were sitting in the library and refusing to leave the building. The police were not gentle. The direct action takes part toward the end of the segment, but the entire video, by Rachel Maddow, is well worth watching.[38]

April 27, 2011 at Hancock Air Base near Syracuse, NY, Thirty-seven arrested as they protest use of Drones.[39]

Imagine if we were to go to all the legislatures, local and national, all events where officials gather, and wherever there is injustice—and let the gangsters and mobsters there who are robbing and murdering not only us, but also at least seven generations after us, know that we are there not only watching them but also resisting in real time. We must heal our country and our beloved and beautiful planet Earth.

This article originally appeared in DailyCensored, 27 April, 2011 (http://www.dailycensored.com/2011/04/27/down-the-rabbit-hole-with-democracy-and-three-urgent-pleas/).

Endnotes

[1] "Tunisian gender-parity 'revolution' hailed" Aljazeera.com, 21 April, 2011 <http://www.aljazeera.com/news/africa/2011/04/2011421161714335465.html>.

[2] Renée Loth, "An uprising for women's rights too," *Boston Globe*, Op-Ed, 16 April, 2011.

[3] Juan Cole and Shahin Cole, "Tomgram: Shahin and Juan Cole, The Women's Movement in the Middle East," Tomdispatch,com, 26 April, 2011 <http://www.tomdispatch.com/post/175384/>.

[4] "Presidential Election, 2 November 2004," OSCE (Organization for Security and Co-operation in Europe), Office for Democratic Institutions and Human Rights, 2004 <http://www.osce.org/odihr/elections/usa/presidential_2004/>.

[5] Center for Hand-Counted Paper Ballots <http://www.handcountedpaperballots.org/>.

[6] Michelle Alexander, *The New Jim Crow: Mass Incarceration in the Age of Colorblindness,* The New Press, New York and London, 2010.

[7] Charles Ogletree, *The Presumption of Guilt: The Arrest of Henry Louis Gates, Jr. and Race, Class and Crime in America,* Palgrave MacMillan, USA, 2010.

[8] Buffy Sainte-Marie, *"My Country 'Tis Of Thy People You're Dying,"* <http://www.metrolyrics.com/my-country-tis-of-thy-people-youre-dying-lyrics-buffy-saintemarie.html>.

[9] "Markey Introduces Nuclear Safety Legislation In Wake Of Japanese Nuclear Meltdown," markey.house.gov, 29 March, 2011 <http://markey.house.gov/bill/2011-nuclear-safety-legislation> and as of 05 July, 2012 <http://markey.house.gov/press-release/markey-statement-fukushima-nuclear-accident-independent-investigation-commission>.

[10] David Coombs, "Message from Bradley Manning's Attorney," couragetoresist.org/bradley-manning, 12 June, 2012 <http://couragetoresist.org/bradley-manning/954-msg-david-coombs-jun12.html>.

[11] Joe Gerstein, "Army Moving WikiLeaks Suspect Bradley Manning to Leavenworth," Politico.com/Under The Radar, 19 April, 2011 <http://www.politico.com/blogs/joshgerstein/0411/Army_moving_Wikileaks_suspect_Bradley_Manning_to_Leavenworth.html>.

[12] "Health Risks Associated with GMOs," Institute for Responsible Technology, <http://www.responsibletechnology.org/health-risks>.

[13] "Organic Consumers Association's Truth-In-Labeling Petition," Millions Against Monsanto <http://www.organicconsumers.org/monsanto/action.cfm>.

[14] Institute for Responsible Technology <http://www.responsibletechnology.org /gmo-basics/gmos-in-food >.

[15] Tom Philipott, "USDA moves to let Monsanto perform its own environmental impact studies on GMOs," Grist.org <http://grist.org/industrial-agriculture/2011-04-19-usda-to-let-monsanto-do-own-environmental-impact-studies-on-gmos>.

[16] Votescam.org <http://www.votescam.org>.

[17] "Maddow & Scarborough: Two Views Of The 'Brooks Brothers Riot' Of 2000," MSNBC's The Rachel Maddow Show (aired: 08/04/09) and Joe Scarborough from Morning Joe (aired: 08/06/09) <http://www.youtube.com/watch?v=ji_k0iORUZg>.

[18] David Barstow and Don Van Natta Jr.,"Examining the Vote; How Bush Took Florida: Mining the Overseas Absentee Vote," The New York Times, 15 July, 2001; pp. A1, A17, A18, <http://www.nytimes.com/2001/07/15/us/examining-the-vote-how-bush-took-florida-mining-the-overseas-absentee-vote.html?pagewanted=1>.

[19] See "*Chapter II: What Went Wrong in Ohio and Black Box Voting.*"

[20] See "*Chapter II.*"

[21] "Election Recount Procedures," Wisconsin Government Accountability Board <http://gab.wi.gov/sites/default/files/publication/65/recount_manual_23968.pdf>.

[22] Jason Stein and Bill Glauber, "Candidates reach recount deal," Wisconsin Journal Sentinel, JSonline, 21 April, 2011 <http://www.jsonline.com/news/statepolitics/120373999.html>.

[23] The Voting News <http://thevotingnews.com/state/wisconsin/>.

[24] "Bush *Et Al v.* Gore, ET AL, Certiorari To The Supreme Court Of Florida, 531 U.S. 98 (2000)," Justia.com <http://supreme.justia.com/cases/federal/us/531/98/case.html>.

[25] Paul Lehto, J.D.,"Bush v Gore and the Supreme Court as Election Terminator," Center for Hand-Counted Paper Ballots <http://www.handcountedpaperballots.org/documents/election_2000.html>.

[26] Al Gore, "2000 Election Concession Speech," 13 December, 2000, <http://www.historyplace.com/speeches/gore-concedes.htm>.

[27] Jeffrey Toobin, The Nine: Inside the Secret World of the Supreme Court (New YorkAnchor Books, A Division of Random House, Inc., 2008). Prologue, pp 1-9; PART TWO, Chapters 11, 12, 13, pp. 165-208.

[28] Sen. Barack Obama's Acceptance Speech in Chicago, Ill., 5 November, 2008, <http://www.washingtonpost.com/wp-dyn/content/article/2008/11/05/AR2008110500013.html>.

[29] Chidanand Rajghatta, "US seeks India role in Egypt elections," The Times

of India, 14 February, 2011 <http://articles.timesofindia.indiatimes.com/2011-02-14/india/28545942_1_strategic-dialogue-tri-valley-students-foreign-secretary>.

[30] "EC seeks roadmap for EVM with printers," Hindustan Times, 15 April, 2011 <http://www.hindustantimes.com/India-news/NewDelhi/EC-seeks-roadmap-for-EVM-with-printers/Article1-685800.aspx>.

[31] The Center for Hand-Counted Paper Ballots <http://www.handcounted-paperballots.org/>.

[32] Vote Rescue <http://voterescue.org/>.

[33] Kim Zetter, "Vote-PAD Rocks the Disabled Vote," Wired.com, 19 January, 2006 <http://www.wired.com/science/discoveries/news/2006/01/70036>.

[34] Douglas Jones, "Voting on Paper Ballots," The University Of Iowa Department of Computer Science <http://www.divms.uiowa.edu/~jones/voting/paper.html>.

[35] Sheila Parks, "Hand-Counted Paper Ballots in 2008," Tikkun.org <http://www.tikkun.org/article.php?story=20090327095732653>. An updated version of this article appears as *"Chapter III: Hand-Counted Paper Ballots Now."*

[36] Humberto Sanchez, "House Passes 2012 Budget resolution," National Journal.com, April 15, 2011 <http://nationaljournal.com/house-gop-passes-2012-budget-resolution-20110415>.

[37] "Where's Our Change" a song to President Obama (Protest song for the 04.21.2011 Breakfast with Obama staged by the Fresh Juice, freshjuiceparty.com, Party) 21 April, 2011 <http://www.youtube.com/watch?v=5uhKYQo5AqQ>.

[38] Rachel Maddow, The Rachel Maddow Blog <http://www.msnbc.msn.com/id/26315908/vp/42725827#42725827>. Wait until the video loads in upper right hand corner of screen.

[39] Dave Tobin, "37 people who protest at Hancock Air Base near Syracuse against the use of drones are arrested Friday," The Post Standard, April 22, 2011 <http://readersupportednews.org/off-site-news-section/44-44/5721-37-arrested-at-hancock-air-base-protesting-use-of-drones>.

V

Wisconsin: Democracy in Our Hands

I cannot watch enough videos of the people in Wisconsin as you bold, brave, most decent Wisconsonites are out in the streets—resisting, doing non-violent civil disobedience/direct action, dissenting, protesting, rising up, standing up to and speaking and singing truth to power in the face of Walker and his cronies.

What is happening in Wisconsin now is a model for the whole country. Not only your honorable actions, but also what Walker and the thugs behind him are trying to do in Wisconsin.

I am writing to tell you not only how much I respect and admire you, but also how very concerned I am about the recalls, scheduled as of this writing to start on July 12. They are to be done on the same electronic voting machines that could have rigged the elections in the first place as well as the Supreme Court recount. For information on hacking of all electronic voting machines by geeks, professors and students—both optical scammers (not a typo) and DRE's/touchscreens—to say nothing of all the fraud and error of the electronic voting machines in real time—some lowlights: FL 2000, GA 2002, OH 2004, the list goes on and on, see the endnotes.[1]

I implore you to do everything you possibly can and then some to have all these recalls hand-counted, in publicly observed, secure hand-counted paper ballots elections. That is the only way to be sure that each one of our votes is counted as cast.

Lawyers right now are exploring the possibility of emergency measures to hand-count all the recalls—but more assistance is needed. Are there any lawyers out there who could help?

An injunction to preserve the evidence is what Corwin[2] did in New York (NY-26) to bar certification of any results and impound all voting equipment and ballots immediately after the election. The Impound Order is part of the link. It is legal to do this in Wisconsin. Given the fact that Wisconsin statutes[3] (See especially Sections 5.05, 5.06 (1), 5.06 (2), 5.06 (8),5.08) clearly allow challenges to elections, voter registration and candidate qualifications, then clearly there needs to be preservation of records in the recalls—ballots, records and other evidence, including the electronic voting machines. The same reasoning that applied in NY-26 governs Wisconsin. I am looking at this from the perspective of a reasonable judge. Any voter can seek an injunction preserving evidence that might substantiate the claim of election fraud. These are highly contested elections. There could be misconduct on the part of election officials. There is potential for some kind of fraud that election officials can't detect. It would be very powerful for a candidate to seek an injunction. Democratic candidates running against the six Republicans who have been recalled are: SD 02 Nancy Nusbaum; SD 08 Sandra Pasch; SD 10 Shelly Moore; SD 14 Fred Clark; SD 18 Jessica King; SD 32 Jennifer Schilling. Democratic candidates who have been recalled by the Republicans are: SD 12 Jim Holperin; SD 22 Bob Wirch; SD 30 Dave Hansen. Ask the candidate where you live to seek an injunction, as Corwin (R) did in NY.

At the Public Hearing at the Wisconsin State Capitol in Madison, Wisconsin, at the Assembly Committee on Election and Campaign Reform on June 10, 2011 this most extraordinary comment by Representative John Pridemore (R-Hartford).

PRIDEMORE: "I will say that I agree with your [Barbara With] position in terms of knowing what I do about voting machine technology and the age of the technology that is in some of our machines. It can [sic] some machines can be programmed to count inaccurately…and they can be programmed to, uh, for instance, uh, two candidates in order to maintain a zero count can be programmed by adding votes to one candidate and subtracting votes. In other words, starting out at a positive and negative number even before the first ballot goes in the machine. And then you can zero out the count and then it will look like zero and looks like everything's correct; but embedded in the programming are numbers that, uh, would offset each other's total as the ballots come in. So it is possible on old technology, and that's why when I mention hard-wired electronics voting machines, that would prevent that from happening. So I want to assure you that, uh, new technology, uh, has taken in those possibilities. In [sic] factored in those possibilities—In the specification that this task force hopefully will write and eliminate that potential for voter fraud."[4]

If this is what Pridemore knows, why would any Wisconsin voter want their vote counted now by these electronic voting machines? How can the Government Accountability Board (GAB) allow the use of these electronic voting machines? How can any of the elected officials in any municipality allow these electronic voting machines to be used? How can Pridemore want these electronic voting machines? For clarity: the GAB is the body that decides on election matters in Wisconsin; most other states, if not all others, use the Secretary of State (SOS) as the official election office.

In one of several telephone conversations with Steve Pickett, an Election Specialist at the GAB, Pickett told me that Wisconsin municipalities (there are 1,851 municipalities and 3,600 polling places) can choose their way of voting. When I questioned him further on this, his answer was much less clear. At one point he said that if a voter wanted to get her municipality to go to hand-counted paper ballots, all she had to do was have all the voters request that their ballots be counted by hand. When I pressed him to be clearer on this, I felt his response was not clear at all. When I asked whether this paper ballot would be different from the ballot used on the op scan machines, his answer was not clear. The best I could fathom was, sometimes yes, sometimes no. And that each voter would have to specify their paper ballot be hand-counted. Where this ballot would be placed so that it would be hand-counted remains a mystery to me. This is worth exploring right now for the recalls.

Pickett also added that in municipalities with 7,500 people—**counted by the census so this includes people who cannot even vote!**—voting must be done by electronic voting machines. **One would think that means that any municipality with a 7,499 count by the census could have hand-counted paper ballots elections, if they choose to do so.** Yet, he also commented that if municipalities have the machines, they must use them! Does that mean they cannot change their minds and get rid of all electronic voting machines like Ireland and the Netherlands have already done—and they are not municipalities, they are countries? Is Pickett correct about this? Further, this contradicts what Picket said earlier about people being able to change from machines to hand-counts, just by asking.

Let's Take a Look at the Laws

Recalls happening in municipalities that have more than 7,500 people need to be counted by electronic voting machines, according to Wisconsin Statute 5.40 (1).[5] Here is a direct quote from the Statute: "....every municipality with a population of 10,000 or more before July 1, 1995, or of 7,500 or more thereafter shall require the use of voting machines or electronic voting systems in every ward in the municipality at every election....."

How could such a law—denying people the right to have their ballots hand-counted—be legal? Who made this law—maneuvered and manipulated it—when and why? Moreover, since it is not even based on the population of registered voters, but on the number of people living there, it seems to me to be very off. Does anyone know if other states have such laws, based on total population and not registered voters?

According to Wisconsin Statute 5.40 (5m)[6] "...the governing body of a municipality may petition the board for permission to use paper ballots and voting booths for a specific election, and the board may grant such a request."

This is muddy in several ways. Is the law talking about paperless DRE's/touchscreens that the GAB may give permission to change to optical scan machines, if requested? Or, is the law saying that whether the municipality uses either kind of electronic voting machine, they can petition the GAB for a publicly observed secure hand-counted paper ballots election? Further, is it true that all Wisconsin electronic voting machines have a paper trail?

Let me warn you now, any form of a publicly observed, secure hand-count of paper ballots will be hard to get but we must try. Whether it was the legislature and/or the GAB that enacted Wisconsin Statute 5.40 (1), asking them for permission to rescind it for an election is asking those who put the law in place to get rid of it, which they are very unlikely to do without a strong grassroots movement pressuring them to do so. However, this avenue must be tried. The GAB has already granted such permission to several municipalities. Public pressure has always been what moves the government to do the right thing for we the people.

Is it possible that it could be up to the election officials in each Wisconsin municipality and not the GAB whether a 100% hand-counted voter oversight—checks and balances—audit could be done?

Let me be clear—the absolute best choice for Wisconsin is that each municipality hand-counts the votes as the only count of the recalls. But, if that is not allowed—and because time is of the essence—the next best choice for Wisconsin is a 100% hand-counted voter oversight—checks and balances—audit done at each polling place, immediately after the machine count. This is not a recount.

Why Is This Distinction Important?

Pickett said that asking for the ballots to be hand-counted after the machine count would be considered a recount and that would not be possible without going through all the required channels in the statutes, found in Chapter 9.[7] The 2005 Wisconsin Act 451 explains more. As I write, I am wondering who enacted Chapter 9, and the 451 Act,[8] when and why?

It appears that the GAB could obstruct justice and not allow hand-counts.

But I cannot help but wonder if the municipalities can trump the GAB, and have the final say about what voting and counting method are used?

Pickett said there would be about 50 polling places in the recalls and that each polling place would have about 1,000 registered voters. Let's say we have ten teams of two people, one counter and one observer, and they change roles on the second hand-count. That would be 500 people. Furthermore, Picket added that I could start now looking for 500 people to be on these teams! However, he ominously stated, "It is not going to happen." He meant, I think, not only that we would not find 500 volunteers but also that the law would not let it happen. Let's see about that.

Please, step forward now to be a volunteer hand-counter to do a 100% hand-counted paper ballots count for the recalls or a 100% hand-counted voter oversight-checks and balances-audit of the recalls immediately after the electronic voting machine counting is done in the municipality where you live.

Two groups on the ground in Wisconsin, specifically dedicated to voting rights are WI Citizens for Election Protection[9] and Wisconsin Counts! Protecting Wisconsin Elections.[10]

Because there is only one race on each ballot, it is a very easy and fast hand-count. (Not that a more complicated ballot is hard.) Some municipalities in Wisconsin already hand-count paper ballots.[11] Approach them and see how they can help.

Hand-Counting Methods

"Chapter XII: On-Site Observations of the Hand-Counting of Paper Ballots and Recommendations for the General Election of 2008," provides descriptions of hand-counted paper ballots elections that I observed in real time. This method of hand-counting is called read and tally or read and mark. Scroll down to the section on Acton, ME. They counted almost 1,000 ballots twice in four hours and they had seven races and two initiatives to count. In Wisconsin, you have only one race. *"Chapter XIII: Sort and Stack Elections in New Hampshire,"* describes another method to hand-count paper ballots. I asked Picket if there were rules in Wisconsin which stated which method had to be used. There are not. Interestingly enough, as in New Hampshire when I did research there, Pickett did not know what hand-counting protocol the Wisconsin municipalities use.

My quick instructions for conducting publicly observed secure hand-counted paper ballots (HCPB) elections now are:

- Hand-counting is done at the polling place, right after the election

- Is publicly observed

- By teams who come in only to hand-count the ballots and have not been at polls all day

- Live-streamed

- Video taped by a designated professional videographer from each opposing party and any other people who want to do so

- Done twice and results must match

- Poll books of voters checking in and poll books of voters checking out must exactly match

- The number of ballots counted must exactly match the number of ballots distributed

- The number of ballots printed must match the number of ballots distributed, voted, and not voted

- Via Jim Mueller: the first thing to do after the polls are closed is to secure all unused ballots, count them and run a 1/4 inch or larger drill bit through them several times in the area for initials

- Make sure that people from both parties observe—with eagle eyes—the taking of the voted and counted ballots out of the op scan machines and putting them out on tables to be hand-counted

- Pickett also brought up the issue of using the AutoMARK electronic voting machine for people with disabilities, stating that anyone who wants to use this machine must be allowed to. This is not acceptable. The AutoMARK must be used only by people with disabilities to keep out any possible rigging this way

- Wisconsin has 22 municipalities who have purchased Vote-PAD, an instrument that provides a means for people with disabilities to mark a ballot without requiring the use of electronic voting machines. These municipalities are in four counties: Adams, Price, Buffalo, Iron. These are the 22 municipalities in WI that have a Vote-PAD.[12] Contact them to borrow their Vote-PADs for the recalls if they are not using them.

Please see *"Chapter IV: Down the Rabbit Hole with Democracy and Three Urgent Pleas"* in this book for a very comprehensive list of elements necessary for secure hand-counted paper ballots (HCPB) elections, scroll down to the third urgent plea.

Preparing for a Recall

Before the recalls, here are some must do's.

- Go door-to-door or call in every municipality where there are recalls
- Give out information about candidates you want people to vote for
- In Wisconsin, people do not register as Democrats or Republicans or any party; observers lists will, therefore, contain all the people registered to vote in each municipality
- Ask people to speak their name very loudly when they are at the polling place checking in
- Ask them to look at the observers when they say their name
- It is legal for each party on the ballot to have a minimum of one observer in each polling place, and more if space allows
- These observers check off voters who come to vote as the poll workers check them in
- This checking off allows the parties to call voters who don't come to vote to see if they need a ride or baby-sitter or something to help them get to the polls
- This list of people that the observers have, checking off who comes to vote, gives the parties an easy check to see if those who responded door-to-door or by telephone of who they would vote for matches the votes cast at the polling place
- For example, if responses door-to-door or by calling resulted in 300 people saying they were going to vote for Jane Doe, and these names are noted on your sheet, and these 300 people show up to vote again and 100 ballots were counted for Jane Doe, something is probably very fishy
- Of course, not all people will tell you at their door or on the phone who they are going to vote for, but many will, and a large discrepancy between that telling and your checking is a huge red flag

My Urgent Plea to You

Over and over again in my head I am hearing, thinking and saying with you: "This is what democracy looks like" and "the whole world is watching." Both are true, you bold, brave, most decent, honorable people of Wisconsin. Keep on keeping on and resisting, doing non-violent civil disobedience/direct action, dissenting, protesting, rising up, speaking and singing truth to power, standing up to Walker and his cronies.

The Human Touch

>Use your hands
>Hoe the garden row
>Awake the wooden rake
>Use your hands
>Hold the child close
>Write letters with pens
>Travel by foot
>Count votes by hand[13]

"Wisconsin, Don't Let Them Rig the Recall!" is an important open letter to the activists of Wisconsin, by my friend and colleague Victoria Collier.[14] Please read it.

Take a stand and count by hand.
In solidarity and with great respect and admiration,

Sheila Parks, Ed.D.

Thanks to Carol Goldman, Deirdre Doran, Dorothy Shubow Nelson, Hannah Miyamoto (retired Wisconsin attorney), Jen Miller, Kevin R. Kratsch, Lucius Chiaraviglio, Marguerite Rosenthal, Priscilla Gebre-Medhin, Steve Pickett, Victoria Collier, Virginia Martin.

This article originally appeared in DailyCensored, 23 June, 2011 (http://www.dailycensored.com/2011/06/23/wisconsin-democracy-in-our-hand/). Updated 30 August, 2012.

Endnotes

[1] Sheila Parks, "Hacking the Machines," Center for Hand-counted Paper Ballots <http://www.handcountedpaperballots.org/documents/Hacking_the_Machines.html>.

[2] Eric Kleefeld, "Corwin Gets Pre-Emptive Legal Action In NY-26," tpmdc. talkingpointsmemo, 24 May, 2011 <http://tpmdc.talkingpointsmemo.com/2011/05/corwin-gets-pre-emptive-legal-action-in-ny-26.php>.

[3] "Chapter V: Elections—General Provisions; Ballots And Voting Systems," Act 451, Wisconsin Stats Database <http://docs.legis.wisconsin.gov/statutes/statutes/5.pdf>.

[4] Transcription by Jim Mueller of Wisconsin.

[5] "2010 Wisconsin Code, Chapter 5. Elections--general provisions; ballots and voting systems., 5.40 Use of voting machines or systems," Justia.com <http://law.justia.com/codes/wisconsin/2010/5/5.40.html>. Here is the current version: <http://law.justia.com/codes/wisconsin/2011/>.

[6] "2010 Wisconsin Code, Chapter 5."

[7] "Chapter 9: Post-Election Actions; Direct Legislation," Wisconsin Stats Database <http://docs.legis.wisconsin.gov/statutes/statutes/9.pdf>.

[8] "2005 Wisconsin Act 451: Administration of Elections and Other Election Provisions," Wisconsin Legislative Council Information Memorandum <http://legis.wisconsin.gov/lc/publications/im/im_2006_04.pdf>.

[9] Wisconsin Citizens for Election Protection <https://www.facebook.com/groups/170172289711561/>.

[10] Wisconsin Counts! Protecting Wisconsin Elections <https://www.facebook.com/groups/111857248934825/>.

[11] Verifiedvoting.org, list of hand-counted paper ballots in Wisconsin municipalities, <http://www.verifiedvoting.org/verifier/searched.php?ec=allall&state=WI&equipment_type%5B%5D=Hand+Counted+Paper+Ballots&vendor%5B%5D=All+Vendors&model%5B%5D=All+Models&vvpat=all&submit=Search&rowspp=50&topicText=&stateText=>.

[12] Verifiedvoting.org, list of WI municipalities using Votepad for people with disabilities, <http://www.verifiedvoting.org/verifier/searched.php?ec=allall&state=WI&equipment_type%5B%5D=Accessible+Ballot+Marking+Device&vendor%5B%5D=Vote-PAD&model%5B%5D=Vote-PAD+Ballot+Marking+System&vvpat=ballot&submit=Search&rowspp=50&topicText=&stateText=>.

[13] © Dorothy Shubow Nelson, March 2011, written expressly for Center for

Hand-Counted Paper Ballots.

[14] Votescam.org <http://www.votescam.org/wisconsin_don_t_let_them_rig_the_recalls>.

VI

Hacking the Recalls: Why We Must Have Hand-Counted Paper Ballots and Citizen Exit Polls

by Grant W. Petty and Sheila Parks, Ed.D.

It goes without saying that the outcomes of the nine Senate recall elections scheduled in Wisconsin will be of intense interest to most of the UW-Madison community. Forecasting the outcome of elections weeks in advance is always a risky business; nevertheless, we offer the following bold prediction:

In at least some cases, the candidate receiving the lesser of the actual votes cast—perhaps, in fact, the candidate *you* passionately opposed—will be declared the official victor.

Chances are, you either think we are nuts or you are already upset with the dismal state of elections in Wisconsin, if not the country. Either way, we hope this article will change your view of both (a) the security of the elections and (b) the ability of ordinary citizens like you to improve that security.

Here's a second prediction which gets to the heart of the real problem: *no one*—not the Government Accountability Board, not the media, not any elected official, and most certainly not *you*—has the slightest hope of ever *disproving* our first prediction in light of current election procedures and practices.

While our first prediction is open to debate, the second is rock solid. Why? Because our appallingly compromised election procedures in this state are simply incapable of detecting or preventing election fraud, due to a combination of wholly inadequate statutory safeguards and criminally negligent enforcement.

(Note by the way, that we are not talking about *voter* fraud, which was ostensibly the reason behind the recently enacted voter ID law. Both the prevalence and practical significance of *voter* fraud is a discredited myth.[1]

If you want your candidate to win an election dishonestly, it is far easier and more effective to *rig the counting of the ballots on the electronic voting machines*. We find it interesting and significant that those in the Wisconsin Legislature who rammed through the voter ID law have so little to say about the far greater threat of election fraud.)

Election fraud is not just a hypothetical concern. In addition to strong circumstantial evidence in countless other cases, instances of clear fraud have been uncovered that led to actual indictments in Cuyahoga County, Ohio,[2] and Clay County, Kentucky.[3] Echoes of Cuyahoga can be heard (by those inclined to hear them) in the recent Waukesha recount.

Experts on election integrity have been sounding two main alarms for at least ten years: (1) it's far too easy to rig elections in ways that are difficult to detect, and (2) there is considerable circumstantial evidence that it is regularly occurring.

Consider this: approximately 1.48 million votes were cast in the Prosser v. Kloppenburg election. The final published difference between them was a mere 7,004 votes, so flipping only 3,502 of them could have given the election back to Kloppenburg. That's only a single vote flipped (or, alternatively, two Prosser votes simply discarded) per 422 cast!

Now consider this: electronic voting machines use proprietary software to tabulate votes. *Not even election officials are allowed to view or test the integrity of the software or the memory cards.* The counting of votes simply *cannot* be observed or verified by the voting public or the election officials. It is impossible to know whether it is being done correctly and honestly. We are being told to take it on faith that the voting machine vendors, and those who have access to the machines, are honest. This is not merely risky, *it is fundamentally antithetical to democracy.*

The Emmy-nominated documentary *Hacking Democracy*[4] presents a shocking demonstration of how easily electronic votes can be hacked, and it also offers troubling evidence that election rigging is *actually occurring*. Even if you don't read beyond this point, please view *Hacking Democracy* and urge family, friends, and acquaintances to watch it as well. You will never view our elections or electronic voting machines the same way again.

We're accustomed to hearing the phrase "innocent until proven guilty" applied to suspects being tried for crimes, and that's as it should be. But we in the United States, more so than in many other developed countries, inappropriately apply the same standard of evidence to our elections. Our naive assumption is that unless unambiguous evidence of fraud or gross error is actually uncovered, it most likely didn't occur. If you can't see it, it must not exist. This is what those who corrupt the election process count on.

Election fraud, like any crime, requires both motive and opportunity. And ample motive can already be found on either side of the current ideological divide in our country.

Imagine the zealous conservative who sincerely believes that abortion is murder and that liberal politicians are therefore condoning murder on a large scale. Or imagine the zealous liberal who sincerely believes that conservative policies will condemn the earth to perish, and soon, from runaway greenhouse warming. Either of these individuals might be persuaded that it's *morally justified and urgently necessary* to commit election fraud in defense of humankind.

Would anyone who cares about honest elections deliberately put either person in charge of actually overseeing and enforcing election procedures? But that's exactly what we do with our partisan elections for county clerks!

As we saw in the last recount, many judgment calls were made as to which ballots would be declared valid and which discarded. And whenever judgment is in play, so is bias. If you are unfortunate enough to live in a county or municipality where your election officials oppose the party or candidate you support, you should be very, very concerned about whether your vote will be fairly counted.

But it doesn't stop at the county level. Consider further the wealthy industrialist who quite plausibly believes that if a certain pro-regulation candidate for Congress loses, s/he and their allies stand to make millions of dollars more per year. Might s/he not be tempted to invest considerable political and financial capital in getting voting machines adopted that can be easily and undetectably hacked? Would they perhaps even get into the business of building them?

We may never be able to eliminate the motive, but we can, and we must, identify and eliminate the *opportunities* to undetectably rig our elections. Until we do, we *cannot* rationally assume that elections are clean and fair. And we therefore *cannot* rationally trust the official outcomes of elections.

Here, in summary, are the major weak links in Wisconsin elections:

Vote Tabulation

Can we be certain votes are being honestly and correctly tabulated by electronic devices? *No.* Unfortunately, current procedures and the electronic voting machines themselves provide absolutely no way to independently verify the accuracy of electronic vote counts short of a full hand-recount of paper ballots. And by Wisconsin law, *most of the recount must be done on the same electronic voting machines that could have been hacked in the first place*. Be aware that the memory and printouts can be made to differ from the real voter intent and that the pre-election testing is useless for detecting fraudulent programming!

Also, although required by Wisconsin law, touch-screen machines used in some districts were found to provide *no* paper record and thus no voter-verifiable (or recountable) record of the vote!

Chain of custody

For the purposes of a recount, are we ensuring that ballots can't be added or subtracted between the time they are cast by the voter and the time they are recounted? As we clearly saw in the recent Wisconsin Supreme Court recount, the mandated procedures for our elections are not always followed. Citizen observers witnessed a stunning range of abnormalities in the labeling/sealing of ballot bags[5] and even discovered a poll tape dated March 30, days before the election.[6] The poll tape in question, with its time stamp of 1:40 AM, was sworn to as actual votes. This claim was later retracted only when persistently questioned.

We have sampled just some of the evidence suggesting that the upcoming recall elections in Wisconsin cannot, and should not, simply be trusted to be honest. Now we come to the most important part: What can still be done to restore confidence in the outcomes?

There are in fact a number of effective steps that can still be taken. All of them require citizen engagement.

1. Wisconsin Citizens for Election Protection[7] are urging hand-counts for the recalls. They have sent letters to all the clerks asking that they hand-count the recalls.[8] You can contact them at protectwi@gmail.com.

2. Contact your county and municipal clerks, election inspectors and the mayor and councilpersons or the town chair and the supervisors. They can authorize the little extra money that it would take to hand-count paper ballots (HCPB)[9] for the recalls in your municipality. Talk to them about the many jurisdictions in Wisconsin[10] and elsewhere that already count their ballots by hand. Acton, Maine[11] (with seven races and two initiatives, six teams of two people each —a Republican and a Democrat—were able to hand-count, twice, 944 ballots in four hours) and Lyndeborough, New Hampshire[12] are potential models for the rest of the country.

3. Volunteer[13] to serve in non-partisan citizen exit polls being organized by the Election Defense Alliance to rigorously and independently verify vote tabulations and chain-of-custody of ballots.

Our final prediction: Unless the Wisconsin recalls are hand-counted in every race, with secure hand-counted paper ballots (HCPB) elections, at least some of them *will* be rigged, with major implications for the balance of power in the Statehouse.

Alarmist? Perhaps. But the only way to be *certain* is to act immediately to close the massive security holes in our elections. Please use social media to share the information described here, and help educate those who naively think that outcome of the recall elections depends solely on getting out the vote, who votes and how they vote.

Protecting election integrity is not 'left' or 'right.' If any commentator or political leader actively objects to making our elections more secure, please ask yourself what their *real* stake is in the current deeply flawed system.

"I consider it completely unimportant who in the party will vote, or how; but what is extraordinarily important is this—who will count the votes, and how."—Josef Stalin

Grant W. Petty
Professor of Atmospheric Science
University of Wisconsin-Madison

Sheila Parks, Ed.D.
Founder, Center for Hand-Counted Paper Ballots

© Grant Petty and Sheila Parks, 2011. This article may be reproduced in whole or part with attribution of authorship and a link to this article.

This article originally appeared in Sifting and Winnowing, 09 July, 2011 (http://siftingandwinnowing.org/2011/07/09/hacking-the-recalls-why-we-must-have-hand-counted-paper-ballots-and-citizen-exit-polls/).

Endnotes

[1] Lorrainne C. Minnite, <u>The Myth of Voter Fraud</u>, (Cornell Univ. Press, 2011)

[2] "Cuyahoga County Election Scandal," Youtube.com <http://www.youtube.com/watch?v=O38UDMzd1T8>.

[3] Brad Friedman "KY Election Officials Arrested, Charged With 'Changing Votes at E-Voting Machines," Bradblog.com, 19 March, 2009 <http://www.bradblog.com/?p=7001>.

[4] Simon Ardizzone, Russell Michaels and Robert Carrillo Cohen, "Hacking Democracy, A Documentary," "An HBO Original, In Association With Teale-Edwards Productions LLC," Free viewing online (81 min.) <http://archive.org/details/Hacking_Democracy>.

[5] Brad Friedman "Exclusive: City Of Brookfield Ballot Bags Found 'Wide Open' In Waukesha County, WI," Bradblog.com, 05 May, 2011 <http://www.bradblog.com/?p=8511>.

[6] Barbara With testifies before Assembly Committee for Election and Campaign Reform, 11 June, 2011<http://www.youtube.com/watch?v=G3HO1D0DByQ>.

[7] Wisconsin Citizens for Election Protection <http://electionprotectionwisconsin.com/>.

[8] James J. Mueller, "Letter to Municipal Clerk," 01 July, 2011 <http://electionprotectionwisconsin.com/wp-content/uploads/2011/07/JJM-letter-20110701-02.pdf>.

[9] Center for Hand-Counted Paper Ballots, Requirements for Secure Elections <http://www.handcountedpaperballots.org/documents/requirements.html>.

[10] Verifiedvoting.org, list of hand-counted paper ballots by state <http://www.verifiedvoting.org/verifier/searched.php?ec=allall&state=WI&equipment_type%5B%5D=Hand+Counted+Paper+Ballots&vendor%5B%5D=All+Vendors&model%5B%5D=All+Models&vvpat=all&submit=Search&rowspp=50&topicText=&stateText=>.

[11] See *"Chapter XII: On-Site Observations of the Hand-counting of Paper Ballots and Recommendations for the General Election Of 2008,"* and scroll down to Acton, ME.

[12] Nancy Tobi, "Lyndeborough NH passes warrant article prohibiting concealed vote counting by computers or any other method," OpEdNews, 13 March, 2010 <http://www.opednews.com/articles/Lyndeborough-NH-passes-war-by-Nancy-Tobi-100313-550.html>.

[13] Election Defense Alliance <http://electiondefensealliance.org/HelpWI>.

VII

Center for Hand-Counted Paper Ballots Sends Letter to Recall Candidates Regarding Election Protection

Dear [Candidate]

My name is Dr. Sheila Parks, and I am the founder of the national organization, Center for Hand-Counted Paper Ballots, http://www.handcountedpaperballots.org. We work closely with the recently formed grassroots group called Wisconsin Citizens for Election Protection (WCEP) http://www.electionprotectionwisconsin.com. This group of Wisconsin citizens is concerned with protecting the integrity of Wisconsin elections.

Many of them observed the Supreme Court recount and were appalled at what they saw. Although the limited media coverage highlighted the human errors in Waukesha County, there was an overwhelming number of problems in municipalities across the State of Wisconsin.

WCEP organized volunteers to observe poll closing procedures as a way to try to improve the integrity and security of Wisconsin's elections. They placed WI citizen volunteers in each of the nine senate districts for the July 2011 elections. The citizens of Wisconsin are especially concerned with integrity in the election process for the recalls because they all have the potential for being close races.

We are all, local and national groups, especially and very seriously concerned about the integrity of the process in the coming General Election on August 9th.

Therefore, I am asking your campaign to file an injunction immediately to impound all voting equipment and ballots when the polls close on election night. The election materials must be protected in the event of a potential recount or other challenges that could be made about the integrity of the election results. You may remember that recently, the Republicans in New York were granted this same injunction earlier this year. Ultimately, the Republicans lost the strongly-held Republican seat to the Democrat. Your injunction is the senate district's best chance for a fair election.

Here is a quote and some details from a paper I published earlier this summer:

"An injunction to preserve the evidence is what Corwin did in New York (NY-26) to bar certification of any results and impound all voting equipment and ballots immediately after the election. It is legal to do this in Wisconsin. Given the fact that Wisconsin statutes (See especially Sections 5.05, 5.06 (1), 5.06 (2), 5.06 (8),5.08) clearly allow challenges to elections, voter registration and candidate qualifications, then clearly there needs to be preservation of records in the recalls ballots, records and other evidence, including the electronic voting machines. The same reasoning that applied in NY-26 governs Wisconsin. I am looking at this from the perspective of a reasonable judge. Any voter can seek an injunction preserving evidence that might substantiate the claim of election fraud. These are highly contested elections. There could be misconduct on the part of election officials. There is potential for some kind of fraud that election officials can't detect. It would be very powerful for a candidate to seek an injunction."

For more information about the issue in NY and what Corwin did,[1] a link to the Impound Order[2] and the Wisconsin Statutes that show Wisconsin can do what NY did[3] please see the notes at the end of this chapter.

Filing an injunction to protect the election materials on election night is essential to ensuring the integrity of the election results. Extraordinary times call for extraordinary measures.

WCEP has worked tirelessly to communicate with municipality clerks throughout Wisconsin to educate them about the vulnerabilities in the Wisconsin election system. They have continuously reached out to the GAB for the very same reason.

I am eager to know how I may communicate most effectively with candidates. I welcome any questions and feedback you may have. A response from you would be much appreciated.

Please visit the WCEP website at www.electionprotectionwisconsin.com. If you have any questions, you may contact me at sheilaruthparks@comcast.net or Jim Mueller, the attorney for WCEP at jimmueller@charter.net.

Thank you for your time, attention and consideration.

Respectfully,
Sheila Parks, Ed.D.
Founder, Center for Hand-Counted Paper Ballots
http://www.handcountedpaperballots.org/

More Info:

Get involved in the Wave and EDA's 'No More Stolen Elections Campaign' centered around the Wisconsin recall elections on Tuesday, August 9th and 16th!

This article originally appeared in WisconsinWave, 07 August, 2011 (http://wisconsinwave.org/news/center-hand-counted-paper-ballots-sends-letter-all-recall-candidates-regarding-election-protect).

Endnotes

[1] Eric Kleefeld, "Corwin Gets Pre-Emptive Legal Action In NY-26," tpmdc/talkingpointsmemo, 24 May, 2011 <http://tpmdc.talkingpointsmemo.com/2011/05/corwin-gets-pre-emptive-legal-action-in-ny-26.php>.

[2] For a link to the impound order, see <http://www.scribd.com/doc/56182443/Impound-Order-For-Results-In-NY-26-Special-Election>.

[3] Here are the Wisconsin Statutes that show Wisconsin can do what NY did: <http://legis.wisconsin.gov/statutes/Stat0005.pdf>.

VIII

Hacking Our Elections With Big Money and Power

By Michael Collins and Sheila Parks, Ed.D.

The formula for modern elections is simple. Candidates must have significant sums of money to compete in primaries. That means anyone absent real money is left out. More importantly, those with the most money have the biggest advantage. Combining money with favorable media is generally a sure winner. Republican Scott Walker outspent Democrat Tom Barrett by nearly a two to one margin,[1] $11 million to $6.7 million. With one exception, the most expensive races for Wisconsin's legislature were won by the best funded candidates. But money isn't the main problem.

The fundamental problem with campaign financing is not the money itself, it's the commitments firmly attached to the donors. When super wealthy donors like the Koch brothers get involved, you can be sure they expect a return for their investment. Again and again, we see policies flow from donors through their acquired political candidates, back to the original donor group in the form of legislative and regulatory preference.

The US Supreme Court went out of its way to extend this practice with its Citizens United decision. That set the stage for Wisconsin and every other state and Congressional election in 2010. The results are apparent—particularly in Wisconsin—in terms of political offices held and actions on behalf of donors. The response by the citizens of Wisconsin is a major roadblock to the toxic effects of unrestrained money and power on our elections.

Yet even the wonderful Wisconsinites might find their roadblock unable to withstand the influence of big money and power, since most of the recalls in the August 9th General Election, like most elections in the USA, will be counted by electronic voting machines. A privatized electronic voting machine industry owns our elections. In 2004, Wally O'Dell, CEO and Chair of the Board of Diebold, said he would help deliver Ohio to Bush. And he did.

Election fraud has been going on at least since 1970. Read the book

Votescam[2] by the late great brothers, James and Kenneth Collier. The book details the League of Women Voters fraudulently punching holes in punch card ballots, on election night, after the polls have closed. Nina Totenberg and Helen Thomas are among the illustrious media people who chose not to report any of the Colliers' election fraud evidence.

Recently, the US Government appears to be promoting election fraud abroad, with Hillary Clinton "wondering" if India could help Egypt's new democracy.[3] Not only does India use electronic voting machines, but also the worst kind.

All the rights of the world depend on our voting rights. If we lose those, we have nothing, and we have pretty much lost those rights already. We must get rid of the influence of big money and power in our elections. The fraud of the electronic voting machines, coupled with the complicity of the corporate media and the politicians, are not glitches, errors, anomalies. To begin to solve this mess, we must immediately go to publicly observed secure hand-counted paper ballot (HCPB) elections.[4]

"You may say I'm a dreamer…."

Imagine a country where people defeated the big tobacco corporations. It is right here, we did it! Now smoking is being banned inside private apartments and cars in parking lots. It's happening because second-hand smoke seriously harms us all and people took action. Now imagine a country where all electronic voting machines are banned, from California to Massachusetts. We can defeat the electronic voting machine corporations too. Publicly observed secure hand-counted paper ballots (HCPB) elections are the only way to ensure all our precious votes are counted as cast.

©Michael Collins and Sheila Parks, Ed.D., 2011. This article may be reproduced in whole or part with attribution of authorship and a link to this article.

Michael Collins is a writer and researcher. His work can be found at http://www.TheMoneyParty.org and other news and opinion sites on the Internet.

Sheila Parks, Ed.D., has been involved with this wave of voting rights since the 2000 Florida presidential election. She is the founder of the Center for Hand-Counted Paper Ballots, http://www.handcountedpaperballots.org.

This article originally appeared in Justice Rising, Summer 2011 (http://www.thealliancefordemocracy.org/pdf/AfDJR5207.pdf). Updated 03 September, 2012.

Endnotes

¹ For more on the two-to-one fundraising difference between Scott Walker and Tom Barrett, see "Record $37.4 Million Spent In Governor's Race," Wisconsin Democracy Campaign/wisdc.org, 08 February, 2011 <http://www.wisdc.org/pr020811.php>.

² James and Kenneth Collier, Votescam (Victoria House Press, Ecublens-Lausanne, Switzerland, 1992). To read the first six chapters online and order the book go to <http://www.votescam.org/votescam_chapters>.

³ Chidanand Rajghatta, "US seeks India role in Egypt elections," The Times of India, 14 February, 2011 <http://timesofindia.indiatimes.com/india/US-seeks-India-role-in-Egypt-elections/articleshow/7490741.cms>.

⁴ For more information on HCPB see *"Chapter IV: Down The Rabbit Hole With Democracy And Three Urgent Pleas,"* and scroll down to the third urgent plea.

IX

In Honor of the Anniversary of the Wisconsin Uprising, February 11, 2011

Wisconsin: The New Florida and Ohio?

In the 2000 presidential election, Florida needed Katherine Harris (then Florida Secretary of State), Jeb Bush, the Supreme Court Justices—and the connections between them—to put George W. Bush in the White House. See John Nichols *Jews For Buchanan*.[1]

"The optical scan machines in Volusia County, a product of Diebold Corporation, were also key in this election. Alastair Thompson wrote a detailed analysis of the election fraud[2] that went on in Volusia Country on optical scans. His account relies heavily on the original work of Bev Harris in Chapter 13, Security Breaches, in her book *Black Box Voting: Ballot-tampering in the 21st Century*.[3] Read the entire book online. The Emmy nominated documentary *Hacking Democracy*[4] shows Finnish computer expert Harri Hursti hacking the same kind of machines as those used in Volusia County. Harris, who arranged the hacks, stars in the film, as does Kathleen Wynne, one of the first people in the country to call for publicly observed secure hand-counted paper ballots (HCPB) elections.

The Election Assistance Commission (EAC) put out a warning in December 2011 about ES&S DS200 IntElect optical scan electronic voting machines producing errors ***during voting***.[5] [Emphasis mine] These machines were used in **Florida,** Illinois, Indiana, **Ohio,** New York and **Wisconsin.** [Emphasis mine] (For more details, see the notes at this chapter's end on the problems in Cleveland[6] and the subsequent government investigation.[7]) Shockingly, the machines will not be decertified. Said Brian Hancock of the EAC: "Our goal is not to decertify systems. We never want to be in a situation of putting counties in a position where they cannot run an election."[8]

In the 2004 presidential election, George W. Bush needed Kenneth Blackwell (then Ohio Secretary of State and also honorary co-chair of the Committee to Re-elect George W. Bush) to stay in the White House. John Conyers (Democratic Representative from Michigan) in *Preserving Democracy: What Went Wrong in Ohio*, had scathing comments about Blackwell's role, stating that many of the problems in Ohio involved "intentional misconduct and illegal behavior," with Blackwell playing a major role.[9] Read the Conyers Report for more.[10] *What Went Wrong In Ohio* can be purchased at Academy Chicago Publishers. Wally O'Dell, president, chair and CEO of Diebold Corporation at the time and also huge fund-raiser for the re-election of Bush, said he would help deliver Ohio's votes to Bush.[11] Although no Diebold touchscreens were used in Ohio in the 2004 general election, other corporations' touchscreens were—the paperless ES&S iVotronic and Infinity DRE from MicroVote, also paperless. Huge thanks to the generosity and knowledge of Wisconsinite John Washburn, historian and computer expert, for his help about DRE's in Ohio in 2004.

***

Here is a Who's Who guide of public figures and organizations to watch among ultra right-wing operatives who are (trying) to manipulate the electoral process in both state and federal government in Wisconsin and elsewhere.

The question remains: are any of these players the new Harris and/or Blackwell?

Jocelyn Webster is a protégé of Karl Rove and is the new Director of Communications at Wisconsin Department of Administration (DOA).[12] See the notes at this chapter's end for a link to her appointment letter and resume[13] and also, for more on her shenanigans[14] and questionable activies for Walker.[15] Some questions remain:

- How and why did she get this job?
- Did Rove or the Koch Brothers or one of their emissaries tell, oops, ask Wisconsin Governor Scott Walker, now on recall with over one million signatures gathered, to appoint her?

Karl Rove is known as The Architect of George W. Bush's presidential campaigns in 2000 and 2004. Bush's nicknames for Rove are Boy Genius and Turd Blossom—a flower that grows out of dung. The question remains:

- Besides Ms. Webster, what tentacles of Rove are in Wisconsin now?

The Koch Brothers, ultra right-wing businessmen, starring especially in oil, recently convened a "super secret meeting"[16] of billionaires to discuss the 2012 elections. In the 2010 gubernatorial elections, the brothers gave $43,000[17] to ultra right Republican Scott Walker and $87,000[18] to Democrat Andrew Cuomo (now governor of New York). See the Koch Brothers' top policy issues in which they outline strategies for repealing health reform, denying climate change, fighting Wall Street reform, dismantling collective bargaining rights, fighting reductions in carbon emissions, keeping corporate money in elections, fighting Internet neutrality.[19] The questions remain:

- What kind of relationship do Mayor Bloomberg of New York City (who ordered police to evict Occupy Wall [OWS] Street from Zuccotti Park) and Andrew Cuomo have?

- Does Bloomberg also have a relationship with the Koch Brothers?

Scott Walker must be watched also, to put it mildly. Many of his top aides[20] have been charged in a John Doe investigation and one of them, Darlene Wink, is going to spill the beans. How many remains to be seen. (See the notes at this chapter's end for a link to the criminal complaint against Wink.[21]) The timing of a Walker e-mail in the "secret e-mail system"[22] might be suspicious, and he himself is "willingly," he says, talking[23] with the investigators. Attorney Mike Pampatonio, host of Ring of Fire radio show, thinks it is extremely risky for him [Walker] to go in there and act like he is going to hustle them…"[24] Oh, now Walker says he "voluntarily"[25] agreed to talk with the investigation when asked to do so. Ernest Canning on bradblog has written a detailed account of all the goings on.[26] Mary Bottari of the Center for Media and Democracy's PR Watch writes about Walker and his relationships with realtors.[27] The questions remain:

- What is Walker's relationship with the Koch Brothers?

- Who is Walker taking orders from?

The American Legislative Exchange Council (ALEC),[28] founded by the

Koch Brothers, advocates for limited government, free markets and federalism. On its Task and Policy task force web page, ALEC says, "A recent survey of members indicated that tax policy was their top concern. In the most recent legislative session, over 500 bills to lower the tax burden and curb excessive government spending were introduced by ALEC members." ALEC writes boiler plate legislation[29] that states adopt. The questions remain:

- Has Wisconsin adopted, under Scott Walker, any of ALEC's boiler plate legislation?
- And if so, which ones?

Kathy Nickolaus is the Waukesha county clerk who was investigated for her activities around the Supreme Court election and recount in Wisconsin, but she was not prosecuted.[30] (See bradblog and Wisconsin Government Accountability Board GAB.[31]) The questions remain:

- What role will Nickolaus play in the Scott Walker recall?
- What role will Nickolaus play in the 2012 General Election?

During 2011, Minnesota-based Command Central[32] first offered to sell EDGE reconditioned touchscreens (with VVPAT, voter-verified paper audit trail) and INSIGHT optical scan machines to municipalities in Wisconsin. No payment was due until January, 2012. Then, when perhaps Command Central did not have enough takers, the company offered to trade two touchscreens for free[33] in exchange for having the municipality returning to Command Central one optical scan machine that they already owned.

A Customer Database from Command Central[34] that lists their electronic voting machines transactions in Wisconsin in 2011 has been posted online. I obtained this database through a request to Ross Hein and Kevin Kennedy of the Wisconsin Government Accountability Board (GAB). Hein, Campaign Finance and Elections Supervisor at the GAB, sent me the chart. In a phone conversation with him on February 16, 2012, Hein told me that the GAB had requested this information from Command Central. I learned a lot from Hein: The information Command Central sent appears to be incomplete. Very worthy of note and not necessarily obvious in the chart, Hein said that Command Central sold to other municipalities the same INSIGHT optical scan machines that were returned to them by some municipalities in exchange for two free EDGE touchscreens. These machines would be about five to seven years old. The Won Eagle machines are from the nineties. "HMA" after "Won Eagle" stands for hardware maintenance agreement. Imagine the money Command Central will be making from maintaining these old machines. According to John Washburn, electronic voting machines companies make most of their money in maintaining the machines, not in selling them.

Optical scan machines are bad enough. These machines lull people into thinking that because there is a paper trail, the paper ballots can always be counted by hand if something is suspect about the machine count of the election. But with many touchscreens, there is no paper trail at all, and therefore no way ever to count the votes again. And often the paper trail that the touchscreens have is worthless and small and fades.

Wisconsin law requires a voter-verified paper audit trail (VVPAT)Â§5.91 (18), "If the device consists of an electronic voting machine, it generates a complete, permanent paper record showing all votes cast by each elector, that is verifiable by the elector, by either visual or nonvisual means as appropriate, before the elector leaves the voting area, and that enables a manual count or recount of each vote cast by the elector."[35] Some questions remain:

- Why and when did Command Central approach Wisconsin?
- Did Command Central also approach other states?
- If so, what other states and when?
- Were the offers the same as those given to Wisconsin municipalities?
- How did they decide which municipalities in Wisconsin to approach?
- When and why did they change from offering touchscreens to sell to offering a free exchange?
- What are the municipalities who paid saying about their neighbors who paid nothing?

More questions:
- Are there connections between the burning issue[36] of a huge open-pit iron mine on the shores of Lake Superior[37] and the electronic voting machines offers of Command Central? As the Bad River Band of the Lake Superior Tribe of Chippewa Indians[38] and other Wisconsin activists protest the proposed mine, police take Sam Morris of the Bad River Band out of the Capitol for drumming.[39] See the notes at

this chapter's end for a link to a press release by the Bad River Band about the International Ecological Treasure[40] that would be destroyed by the proposed mine.

- Are there connections between the municipalities that accepted for free or bought Command Central offer and the iron mines?

- Is there no connection to the iron mines issue of those municipalities that refused the offer?

- Why did some of the municipalities refuse the deal?

More questions, these from attorney Jim Mueller of Wisconsin Citizens for Election Protection, a Facebook group you can join.[41]

- What are specific municipalities Command Central contracts with?

- Who are the principals of Command Central and what are their political, financial and criminal backgrounds?

- Who are the programmers and what are their political, financial and criminal backgrounds?

- Where did Command Central get the machines? From some state banning them out?

- How can Command Central give two machines in exchange for one twenty-year-old machine?

- What is their fee structure for programming, supplying and maintaining the machines?

- What operating instructions do they give to election officials?

- Who owns the owner of Command Central?

Bottom line, who is Command Central?[42] In private Facebook communications and on the telephone in February 2012, in response to questions I had asked him, John Washburn told me that Command Central has been in Wisconsin for twenty years and is the exclusive distributor for Dominion Voting Systems in Wisconsin, Minnesota, the Dakotas, and Michigan. The question remains:

- Is there a connection between the offers of Command Central and the desire to rig the upcoming Scott Walker recall and also the 2012 General Election?

Electronic voting machines and the rigged elections coming from them are pushing this country not only to the right, but to the ultra right. I do not believe the people of the USA, the 99%, are ultra right. Since the passage of the Help America Vote Act (HAVA)—a well thought out and planned strategy to steal our elections—most jurisdictions/municipalities across the country use electronic voting machines for voting. Verified Voting periodically publishes a fantastically helpful listing of all election equipment used in jurisdictions in the USA; see Election Equipment 2012.[43]

Whether Direct Recording Electronic (DRE)/touchscreens or optical scans, all electronic voting machines can be, and have been, hacked. Many states are still using touchscreens that do not even have a paper trail. Paper ballots, as used with optical scan electronic voting machines, of themselves are not enough. Paper ballots are not very valuable unless they are hand-counted in publicly observed secure elections. How many recounts have their been? And how many changed the result of the election?

There have been only two notable hand-recounts. The first was the hand-recount in Washington state in 2004, which overturned the machine election results and gave Christine Gregoire the governor's seat. The second was the hand-recount in Minnesota in 2008, when the electronic voting machines count was overturned and Al Franken won the Senate seat in the hand-recount. Several years ago, in a telephone conversation with voting rights activist Paul Lehto, he stated that in both cases the recounts were for Democratic candidates and both states had a sympathetic Democratic governor who supported the recount.

The words "paper ballots" obfuscate the issue to the uninitiated. The solution to the fraud and error associated with all electronic voting machines, is elections counted and decided by publicly observed, secure hand-counted paper ballots (HCPB). With that kind of HCPB elections, we have the fairest and most transparent opportunity to know that our votes are counted as cast. See Center for Hand-Counted Paper Ballots[44] for extensive readings bout hacking and the solution.[45]

The Scott Walker recall election must not be rigged.

The 2012 Senate race between Scott Brown and Elizabeth Warren in Massachusetts must not be rigged.

The 2012 General Election must not be rigged.

The bandwagon: Please, get on it with us to struggle for elections decided by publicly observed, secure hand-counted paper ballots (HCPB). If you "like" this Facebook page,[46] Center for Hand-Counted Paper Ballots, you will be able to keep current with information on this endeavor and actions to take. You can also suggest to all of us what you think we can do about this dire situation. We cannot let the 1%, owners of the privatized electronic voting machine industry, or owners of those who own the corporations, continue to rig elections that belong to us, the 99%.

Non-violent resistance: The hard-won victories of the Civil Rights, Women's Suffrage and LGBTQ movements came about not only when people lobbied Congress (local or federal), wrote letters to the editor, held rallies and marches, signed petitions, and donated money. It took much more than that. Non-violent resistance was an integral and vital part of these movements.

We must pay close attention to the Occupies and what they are doing. Do mic checks everywhere. Do everything else you can think of to bring attention to the rigging of our elections and to help change the hearts, minds and souls of people everywhere.

Watch: Cameras: Fantastic You Tube instructions for taking pictures of the revolution,[47] via extraordinary videographer, Nicole Desautels Schulte, on the ground in Wisconsin.

Thank You: Tunisia, Egypt, Wisconsin, Occupies, Deborah Sirotkin Butler, Lucius Chiaraviglio, Michael Collins, Bob Fleischer, Mindy Fried, Brad Friedman, Janet Jesberger, Mary Magnuson, Nina Moliver, Marianne Moonhouse, Jim Mueller, Marguerite Rosenthal, Nicole Desautels Schulte, Joseph Skulan, John Washburn. I am completely responsible for the text and any errors in it. This article may be reproduced in whole or part, with attribution of authorship given and link to this article.

This article originally appeared in DailyCensored, 17 February, 2012 (http://www.dailycensored.com/2012/02/17/in-honor-of-the-anniversary-of-the-wisconsin-uprising-february-11-2011-wisonsin-the-new-florida-and-ohio/). Updated 08 August, 2012.

Endnotes

[1] John Nichols, <u>Jews for Buchanan: Did You Hear the One About the Theft of the American Presidency?</u>, (New Press, 2001)

[2] Alastair Thompson, "Diebold Memos Disclose Florida 2000 E-Voting Fraud," Scoop Independent News, 24 October, 2003 <http://www.scoop.co.nz/stories/HL0310/S00211.htm>.

[3] Bev Harris, <u>Black Box Voting: Ballot-tampering in the 21st Century</u>, (Talion Publishing, March 2004); particularly Chapter 13, "Security Breaches." The entire work can be read online at <http://www.blackboxvoting.org/bbv_chapter-13.pdf>.

[4] SimonArdizzone, Russell Michaels and Robert Carrillo Cohen, "Hacking Democracy, A Documentary," "An HBO Original, In Association With Teale-Edwards Productions LLC," Free viewing online (81 min.) <http://archive.org/details/Hacking_Democracy>.

[5] Gregory Korte, "Federal Agency Finds Defects In Ballot Scanners," USAToday/USAtoday.com, 23 December, 2003 <http://www.usatoday.com/news/politics/story/20-11-12-22/defective-voting-machines/52172034/1?mid=55>.

[6] C. Weiser, "Cleveland Voting Machines Miss Votes, Freeze Up," Cincinnati.com/blogs <http://cincinnati.com/blogs/politics/2011/12/23/cleveland-voting-machines-miss-votes-freeze-up/>.

[7] Laura Johnston, "U.S. Government Investigation Finds Cuyahoga County's Election Machines Are Flawed," <u>Cleveland Plain Dealer.</u> 22 December, 2011 <http://blog.cleveland.com/metro/2011/12/us_government_investigation_fi.html>.

[8] See Gregory Korte, endnote 5.

[9] See *"Chapter II: <u>What Went Wrong in Ohio and Black Box Voting.</u>"*

[10] "Preserving Democracy: What Went Wrong in Ohio," Status Report of the House Judiciary Committee Democratic Staff, 05 January, 2005 <http://www.iwantmyvote.com/lib/downloads/references/house_judiciary/final_status_report.pdf>.

[11] "Wally O'Dell," profile, NNDB <http://www.nndb.com/people/348/000109021/>.

[12] Joe Vittie, "Walker's DOA Attempts to Sell the Constitution," Wisconsinreporters.com, 14 December, 2011 <http://wisconsinreporters.com/subscribe/walkers-doa-attempts-to-sell-the-constitution/>.

[13] Hematite, "Jocelyn Webster files" Wisconsin Citizens Media Co-op, 08 February, 2012 <http://wcmcoop.com/members/jocelyn-webster-files/>.

[14] Brendan Fischer, "Walker Enlists Karl Rove Protégé to Promote New Protest Policy," The Center for Media and Democracy's PR Watch, 16 December, 2011 <http://

www.prwatch.org/news/2011/12/11191/walker-enlists-karl-rove-protege-promote-new-protest-policy>.

[15] Brendan Fischer, "Meet Gov. Scott Walker's New Political Hit Women," Alternet.org, 05 February, 2012 <http://www.alternet.org/story/153979/meet_gov._scott_walker's_new_political_hit_women/?page=entire>.

[16] Lee Fang, "Koch Brothers Convene Super-Secret Billionaires' Meeting for 2012 Elections," Alternet.org/Republic Report, 04 February, 2012 <http://www.alternet.org/story/153998/koch_brothers_convene_super-secret_billionaires%27_meeting_for_2012_elections?page=1>.

[17] Tony Carrk, "The Koch Brothers: What You Need to Know About the Financiers of the Radical Right," Center for American Action Fund, April 2011 <http://www.americanprogressaction.org/issues/2011/04/pdf/koch_brothers.pdf> (p.18).

[18] Carrk 18.

[19] Carrk 2.

[20] Daniel Bice and Dave Umhoefer, "Two ex-Walker Aides Charged With Illegal Campaigning," The Journal Sentinel, 26 January, 2012 <http://www.jsonline.com/news/statepolitics/doe27-6q3v4uj-138159264.html>.

[21] State of Wisconsin Criminal Complaint against Darlene Wink, "Political Solicitation by a Public Employee," Wispolitics.com 26 January, 2012 <http://www.wispolitics.com/1006/120126_Wink_Complaint.pdf>.

[22] John Lounsbury, "Timing of Walker Email Key: Russell Was Not Deputy Chief of Staff, But Running Campaign-At-Work Operation," Uppitywis.org, 29 January, 2012. Originally <http://uppitywis.org/blogarticle/timing-walker-email-key-russell-was-not-deputy-chief-staff-runni>.

[23] Sarah Jones, "Scott Walker Lawyers Up as John Doe Investigation Stalks Wisconsin GOP," Politicsusa.com, 03 February, 2012 <http://www.politicususa.com/en/wisconsin-gop-scott-walker-lawyer>.

[24] "Walker is talking," on The Ed Show, 04 February, 2012 <http://video.msnbc.msn.com/the-ed-show/46260085#46260085>.

[25] "Gov. Walker says DA requested talks on John Doe probe," Associated Press, 06 February, 2012 <http://www.todaystmj4.com/news/local/138802614.html>.

[26] Ernest A. Canning, "Prosecutors May be Closing in on Walker as WI Gov Implicated In Criminal Complaint Against Aides," Bradblog, 13 February, 2012 <http://www.bradblog.com/?p=9114>.

[27] Mary Bottari, "Will Walker's Love Affair with Realtors Come Back to Haunt Him?" The Center for Media and Democracy's PR Watch, 14 February, 2012 <http://www.prwatch.org/node/11296>.

[28] American Legislative Exchange Council, Center for State Fiscal Reform <http://www.alec.org/initiatives/critical-state-fiscal-reform/>.

[29] American Legislative Exchange Council, The Tax and Fiscal Policy Task Force <http://www.alec.org/task-forces/tax-and-fiscal-policy/>.

[30] Brad Friedman, "EXCLUSIVE: WI State Election Board Failed to Review Minutes from Waukesha County 'Recount' Before Certifying Supreme Court Election Results," Bradblog 30 May, 2011 <http://www.bradblog.com/?p=8545>.

[31] Government Accountability Board, State Of Wisconsin, "G.A.B. Releases Report of Independent Investigation into Waukesha County Clerk Kathy Nickolaus," 28 September, 2011 <http://gab.wi.gov/node/2034>.

[32] Command Central Inc., Waite Park, MN, "Special Pricing on Reconditioned Edges and Insights for the 2012 Presidential Election Offer," <http://a5.sphotos.ak.fbcdn.net/hphotos-ak-ash4/403205_273938612672908_100001703145308_703622_1590280061_n.jpg>.

[33] Marianne M. Moonhouse, Maggie Thomas, and Sierra Nolan, "Command Central Offers WI Munis Deals Too Good To Refuse," WI Citizens for Election Protection, 22 November, 2011 <http://www.handcountedpaperballots.org/documents/Wisconsin%20Command%20Central%20muni%20deal.html>.

[34] "Barron County Customer database," Command Central Inc. <http://www.handcountedpaperballots.org/documents/CC%20Additions%20in%202011.pdf>.

[35] WI Statute 5.91, "5.91 Requisites for approval of ballots, devices and equipment," Wisconsin Legislative Documents <http://docs.legis.wi.gov/statutes/statutes/5/III/91>.

[36] Rebecca Kemble, "Wis. Tribes Vow to Fight Walker over Mine," The Progressive/progressive.org, 27 January, 2012 <http://progressive.org/wis_tribes_vow_to_fight_walker_over_mine.html>.

[37] Todd Richmond, "Penokee Hills, Wisconsin Mine: GOP Senators Split Over Bill," Huffingtonpost.com, 16 February, 2012 <http://www.huffingtonpost.com/2012/02/16/penokee-hills-wisconsin-gop-senators-_n_1281684.html?ref=fb&src=sp&comm_ref=false>.

[38] Great Lakes Inter-tribal Council, "Bad River Band of the Lake Superior Tribe of Chippewa Indians," <http://www.glitc.org/pages/brblsc.html>.

[39] "Heartbeat of Red Cliff Band Stifled in Capitol" Youtube.com, 26 January, 2012 <http://www.youtube.com/watch?v=wSNCeWN5ZSE>.

[40] Bad River Chippewa Tribal Site <http://www.badriver-nsn.gov/>.

[41] Wisconsin Citizens for Election Protection, Facebook.com <https://www.facebook.com/groups/170172289711561/>.

[42] Marianne M. Moonhouse, Sierra Nolan and Darcy Gustavsson, "Command Central—Who Are They? Can We Trust Them With Our Votes?" Wisconsin Counts!

Protecting the Walker Recall Election <http://www.handcountedpaperballots.org/documents/Wisconsin%20Command%20Central%20profile.html>.

[43] "Election Equipment 2012," Verifiedvoting.org <http://verifiedvoting.org/verifier/>.

[44] The Center for Hand-Counted Paper Ballots <http://www.handcountedpaperballots.org/index.html>.

[45] Sheila Parks, "Requirements for Secure Elections," The Center for Hand-Counted Paper Ballots, 06 January, 2012 <http://www.handcountedpaperballots.org/documents/requirements.html>.

[46] The Center for Hand-Counted Paper Ballots, Facebook.com <https://www.facebook.com/pages/Center-For-Hand-Counted-Paper-Ballots/247752928605472>.

[47] "Filming a Revolution a Tutorial—Your Camera is your Weapon," Youtube.com <http://www.youtube.com/watch?v=vUMPssUP0bc&feature=youtube>.

*What Does
The War On Women
Have To Do
With This?*

X

Crashing at the Intersection of Women's Rights and Voting Rights

Prologue 1: Enter Rigged Erections

The war on women and war on our ballots via hackable electronic voting machines are inextricably intertwined. These wars are being waged by the same oppressors: the 1% and their tentacles reaching into their flunkies and robots in the 99%. The 1% either own the corporations that own the electronic voting machines or own those people who own the corporations. But take heed, anyone could hack these machines. These oppressors want to control not only the entire country, but also, specifically and especially, women's bodies. They seek this control by restricting and outlawing our reproductive rights, including access to contraception. Not a peep about abolishing insurance coverage for Viagra and rigged erections.

Prologue 2: The Silencing of the Vaginas

The silencing in Michigan of Representative Lisa Brown for saying vagina—VAGINA VAGINA VAGINA—while the men in the room were trying to legislate our vaginas is a new low in the lengths the good old Republican boys will go to in their attempts to control us. As Brown said, "I am outraged that this legislative body not only wants to dictate what women do, but what we can say." As reported recently by Cassie Murdoch on Jezebel.com, Michigan was in the midst of attempting to pass the most restrictive law in the country on abortion rights[1]—so far. Eve Ensler performed *The Vagina Monologues*[2] with Representative Brown and other Michigan representatives in the Capitol building on Monday, June 18.

Prologue 3: Kissing Roe v. Wade Goodbye

The most important and longest lasting action against women by George W. Bush, our selected president, was his packing of the Supreme Court with Samuel Alito and John Roberts. There is the power and the will in the Supreme Court now to overturn Roe v. Wade one step at a time. Roe is already being dismantled, one state at a time.

The Recent War on Women and Reproductive Rights

All these laws are being introduced by Republicans.

In April 2012 I spoke and e-mailed with Elizabeth Nash, the State Issues Manager of the Guttmacher Institute. I learned that the two states where the worst legislation against women has passed are Arizona (Governor Jan Brewer (R) and Kansas (Governor Sam Brownback (R). Arizona legislators passed six major restrictions: limiting how medication for abortion is provided, mandating an ultrasound before an abortion, prohibiting physician assistants and nurses from providing abortions, banning abortions for reasons of race and gender selection, prohibiting the use of public funds or tuition to be used to pay for abortion training at Arizona universities, and banning abortion at 18 weeks post fertilization. Kansas law bans abortion at 20 week post fertilization, has onerous and unnecessary abortion clinic regulations, limits how medication for abortion is provided, prohibits abortion coverage in health plans (except when necessary to save a woman's life), and requires abortion counseling. This counseling must include information that the abortion "will terminate the life of a whole, separate, unique and living human being."

The Guttmacher Institute has posted a state-by-state report of state legislation, enacted in 2012, regarding reproductive rights.[3] Nash said that between 2000 and 2011, the number of states with less intrusive abortion-related policies dropped from 19 to 9, whereas the number of states with laws hostile to reproductive choice increased from 15 to 26. Jezebel.com recently published a terrific article by Erin Gloria Ryan on state by state anti-choice laws enacted in 2012.[4]

In 2010, ultra-right-wing Republican governors were elected in Alabama, Arizona, Florida, Maine, Michigan, New Jersey, Ohio, South Carolina, Texas, and Wisconsin. In several of these states, these governors were not part of a long line of Republican governors. In fact, in some of these states, these governors interrupted a long line of Democratic governors.

Also in 2010, the Republican Party took control of a majority of the state legislative bodies. Nineteen of these state houses went from Democrat to Republican control.

Here in Massachusetts, Scott Brown (R) won Ted Kennedy's (D) seat, and with that vote we lost a supporter of reproductive rights. A Project Vote Smart review of Brown's record on abortion issues reveals[5] that in 2011, NARAL rated him

45% and National Right to Life rated him 75%. In 2010, NARAL rated Brown 0% and in 2009-2010 National Right to Life rated him 100%. See Vote Smart[6] to understand these evaluations.

Americans United for Life (AUL) is the organization that writes templates and boilerplate legislation against abortions and other reproductive rights. AUL specializes in the super-hatred of women and our bodies. Charmaine Yoest, the president and CEO of AUL who influenced the Komen Organization to defund Planned Parenthood, also testified against the appointment of Sonia Sotomayor and Elena Kagan to the Supreme Court.

Reproductive rights, including contraception, are only part of the War on Women. There are other areas where this war is being fought: equal pay, jobs, domestic violence, and education. If we women don't own our own bodies, we have nothing. The recent laws restricting abortions will most heavily affect low-income women, young women, women of color and rural women. Rich women will always have access to abortions.

We have not heard the last of pre-natal personhood (North Carolina, Governor Bev Perdue (D); both legislative chambers Republican) and trans-vaginal ultra sounds (Virginia, Governor Bob McDonnell (R); both legislative chambers Republican). These misogynist crimes against women are two of the most barbarous tools in the war on women currently being perpetrated by the ultra-right wing. Since the Republicans vote in lock-step for these laws, I wonder if there are any who don't subscribe to the ultra-right wing of the Republican party.

Enter Rigged Elections—The War on our Ballots

I still believe that most people do not align with the ultra-right wing (the Tea baggers and the Wisconsin recall results notwithstanding). So how can we explain the shift in the vote to the right wing, represented by the Republican party? As someone who cares deeply about these issues and who has been following them since the 2000 Florida presidential election, I cannot help but conclude that Republicans are rigging elections by means of electronic voting machines. I also cannot help but ask why the Democrats are silent and, therefore, complicit.

Richard Charnin's "Wisconsin Recall: As usual, the Final Exit Poll was forced to match an unlikely recorded vote," provides ground-breaking and brilliant work in an account of what really happened in the totaling of votes in the Wisconsin recall of Governor Scott Walker (R).[7] Charnin talks of "adjusted exit polls", meaning exit polls that the corporate media "adjust" to match the rigged outcome of the elections. Our elections are not owned by the people. Our elections are rigged by a privatized electronic voting machine industry, a few corporations. The people who are behind these corporations promote their hatred of women and control of our bodies via rigged elections.

There is an enormous amount of evidence[8] that electronic voting machines are vulnerable to errors, to hacking, and to fraud, and that such breaches of democratic process have repeatedly occurred. More evidence has been provided by Bob Fitrakis[9] and Brad Friedman.[10] I cannot think of any Democrat who has won an "upset" election since the 2000 presidential election. Can you? I can think of many Republicans who are in office from such "upset" victories. I cannot think of any state or legislative body where the Democrats are in control and where legislation against women gets introduced and passed. Can you?

Some say it can't happen here. But an honest look at U.S. history tells us we have never had democracy for the 99%. First, Europeans came and slaughtered the Native peoples; then, the oppressors enslaved people of African descent (60 million Africans shipped here like cargo from Africa); women did not vote until 1920, and we continue to fight wars all over the world.

Rigging elections is a hydra-headed monster. Voter ID and other means of suppressing the vote of elders, students, and African Americans occurs everywhere, and these measures are mostly, if not entirely, introduced by Republicans. Money and Citizens United also play their part. In Massachusetts in 2010, millions of dollars from out of state poured into Scott Brown's (R) coffers and in the Scott Walker (R) recall in Wisconsin in 2012 millions also poured in from out of state. Yet, even if all the suppression of the vote and the money were stopped immediately, election fraud will continue as long as the electronic voting machines are in use.

Rigging our elections via electronic voting machines allows the ultra-right wing to triumph in its hatred and fear of women and its ardent desire to control us, and few realize that this is going on. All the electronic voting machines are tallied in ways not visible to the human eye and recounts are difficult, if not impossible. How does this work? Direct Recording Electronic (DRE) and touchscreen electronic voting machines often do not have a paper trail at all, so elections cannot ever be recounted. Optical scan machines do have a paper trail, but obtaining a hand recount is expensive and riddled with regulations. Optical scan machines, as well as touchscreens, are susceptible to error, hacking and fraud. *Hand-marked, publicly observed secure hand-counted paper ballots (HCPB) elections are the only way to ensure that our elections are fair and that our precious votes are counted as cast.*

To the Occupy Movement

I know, I know—many people in the Occupy movement and elsewhere see no difference in either major party and say voting is irrelevant. For me, there is a difference even between -1 and 0. I want to know first that our votes are counted as cast, and next who really won the election. On the machines there is no way of knowing. Both DRE's/touchscreens and optical scan electronic voting machines have been hacked by computer scientists, without trace. The Election Assistance Commission (EAC) [an independent agency of the US government, created by the Help America Vote Act—HAVA] put out a warning in December 2011 about ES&S DS200 IntElect optical scan electronic voting machines errors **during voting** [emphasis mine].[11] These machines were used in all or part of **Florida,** Illinois, Indiana, **Ohio,** New York, and **Wisconsin** [emphasis mine]. Read more details on the "Politics Extra" blog at cincinnati.com[12] and in *The Plain Dealer.*[13] Read *"Chapter I: Hacking the Machines,"* about the most noted hacks of electronic voting machines by computer scientists.

Watch *Hacking Democracy*[14] free on your own computer for one of the most famous hacks, done on the same machines on which Volusia County counted its vote in Florida in the 2000 presidential election. In this hack, Harri Hursti also demonstrated that he could go in and tamper with the program of the machine and leave no trace. Read *"Chapter IX: In Honor of the Anniversary of the Wisconsin Uprising, February 11, 2011—Wisconsin: The New Florida and Ohio?"* for a full description of what happened in Volusia.[15]

I love the Occupy movement and am part of Occupy Boston. We in the voting rights movement need you, the Occupy people: your honesty, courage, mic checks, steadfastness, analysis, reaching millions of people, street creds and non-violent civil disobedience. I implore all Occupy people to join us and help stop election fraud, the war on our ballots, and thus also the war on women.

See web site, Center for Hand-Counted Paper Ballots <http://www.hand-countedpaperballots.org/> and our Facebook page <https://www.facebook.com/pages/Center-For-Hand-Counted-Paper-Ballots/247752928605472>.

I am completely responsible for the text and any errors in it. This article may be reproduced in whole or part, with attribution of authorship given and link to this article.

Thank you to all the sisters and brothers fighting both these wars everywhere, Elizabeth Nash, Jackie, Michelle Weiser, Mindy Fried, Nina Moliver, Stephen Caruso.

Bio: Parks, the Founder of the Center for Hand-Counted Paper Ballots and a long-time ardent feminist and internationalist, defended the abortion clinics with her body for a very long time. She does not want to go back to doing that and fervently hopes that those of you who have not had to do so, never have to.

This article originally appeared in OpEdNews, 10 July, 2012 (http://www.opednews.com/articles/Crashing-at-the-Intersecti-by-Sheila-Parks-120710-968.html). Updated 14 July, 2012.

Endnotes

[1] Cassie Murdoch, "Michigan's Extreme Anti-Abortion Bill Leads the Nation in Batshittery," Jezebel.com, 08 June, 2012 <http://jezebel.com/5916818/michigans-extreme-anti+abortion-bill-leads-the-nation-in-batshittery/>.

[2] "Vaginas Take Back the Capitol!" Public Event Posted on facebook.com, Monday 18 June, 2012 <https://www.facebook.com/events/268583796582574/>.

[3] "State Legislation Enacted in 2012 Related to Reproductive Health," Guttmacher Institute/updates, 01 July, 2012 <http://www.guttmacher.org/statecenter/updates/2012newlaws.pdf>.

[4] Erin Gloria Ryan, "A State-By-State Guide to 2012's Anti-Choice Laws (So Far)" Jezebel.com, 11 May, 2012 < http://jezebel.com/5906797/a-state+by+state-guide-to-2012s-anti+choice-laws-so-far/>.

[5] "Senator Scott P. Brown's Special Interest Group Ratings," Project Vote Smart/Interest Group Ratings <http://votesmart.org/candidate/evaluations/18919>.

[6] Project Vote Smart/Interest Group Ratings, scroll way down almost to the bottom of the page to this section "How to Interpret these Evaluations."

[7] Richard Charnin, "Wisconsin Recall: As usual, the Final Exit Poll was forced to match an unlikely recorded vote," Richardcharnin.com, 06 June, 2012 <http://richardcharnin.com/WisconsinRecallExitPoll.htm>.

[8] Center for Hand-Counted Paper Ballots <http://www.handcountedpaperballots.org/index.html>.

[9] Bob Fitrakis "Diebold, Electronic Voting And The Vast Right-Wing Conspiracy," Fraudbusterbob.com, 42 February, 2004 <http://fraudbusterbob.com/blog/2008/11/07/diebold-electronic-voting-and-the-vast-right-wing-conspiracy/>.

[10] Brad Friedman, "Palm Beach Elections Overturned After Hand-Count Reveals Op-Scans Mistallied Results,"Bradblog.com, 20 March, 2012 <http://www.bradblog.com/?p=9221&fb_source=message>.

[11] Gregory Korte, "Federal agency finds defects in ballot scanners," USA TODAY, 23 December, 2011 <http://www.usatoday.com/news/politics/story/2011-12-22/defective-voting-machines/52172034/1?mid=55>.

[12] C. Weiser, "Cleveland voting machines miss votes, freeze up," Cincinnati.com/Politics Extra, 23 December, 2011 <http://cincinnati.com/blogs/politics/2011/12/23/cleveland-voting-machines-miss-votes-freeze-up/>.

[13] Laura Johnston, "U.S. government investigation finds Cuyahoga County's election machines are flawed," Cleveland.com, 22 December, 2011<http://blog.cleveland.com/metro/2011/12/us_government_investigation_fi.html>.

[14] Simon Ardizzone, Russell Michaels and Robert Carrillo Cohen, "Hacking Democracy, A Documentary," "An HBO Original, In Association With Teale-Edwards Productions LLC," Free viewing online (81 min.) <http://archive.org/details/Hacking_Democracy>.

[15] Sheila Parks, "In Honor of the Anniversary of the Wisconsin Uprising, February 11, 2011—Wisconsin: The New Florida and Ohio?" (Second paragraph) OpEdNews, 20 February, 2012 <http://www.opednews.com/articles/IN-HONOR-OF-THE-ANNIVERSAR-by-Sheila-Parks-120219-509.html>.

Hand-Counted Paper Ballots 101

XI

Hand-Counted Paper Ballots: Frequently Asked Questions

Note: the following is based on a document originally prepared in collaboration with Roy Lipscomb.

Glossary: Some Useful Terms to Know

HCPB

Hand-Counted Paper Ballots.

Electronic voting machine

A computer used for collecting and counting votes in the polling place.

DRE

Direct Recording Electronic (a.k.a., touch-screen) voting machine.

Optical scanner voting machine

Opscan (or optiscan), a computer that counts votes by detecting the choices marked on a paper ballot by the voter.

Security

Protection against mistakes, accidents, and fraud.

HAVA

Help America Vote Act, passed by Congress in 2002, intended to upgrade and regulate the voting systems used in the United States.

HCPB Fundamentals

What are HCPB?

Hand-Counted

> Tallied by citizens without the aid of tools other than paper and pencils.

Paper

> A durable medium which allows data to be clearly and permanently inscribed.

Ballot

> A list of contests and the corresponding candidates and initiatives (if any) in an election.

What are the essential elements of HCPB?

- The paper ballot, marked with the voter's choices, is the official record of the voter's choices and is the record used in the official vote counting.
- The citizens who do the hand-counting include representatives from the different parties on the ballot. This provides essential checks and balances on the counting.
- The counting takes place in the polling place immediately after the polls close.

What are the benefits of HCPB?

- Reliable—Other systems rely on HCPB for confirmation of their results.
- Simple—It's less prone to equipment breakdown, poll worker confusion than other systems.
- Easy to use—People without disabilities need only a pen or pencil. People with disabilities can be provided with other appropriate accessories.

- Authoritative—It employs the actual document prepared by the voter, not a reproduction.
- Secure—Once placed in the ballot box, the ballot is inaccessible before the counting.

Why choose HCPB against the recommendation of so many computer experts?

- Many, perhaps most, computer experts prefer HCPB.
- Some computer experts say, "Don't rely on computer experts—not even us!" In other words, evaluate the various systems and see which meets the standards required by a democracy.

Aren't HCPB simply a nostalgic throwback to some idyllic "good old days"?

Not at all. Longing to return to the "old days" before computers existed would be as misguided as longing for some idyllic, electronic paradise where computers are trusted to control every aspect of our lives. Computers are essential to maintaining and improving life and liberty in today's complex world.

Aren't HCPB systems obsolete?

- Our interest is the best way to conduct elections, regardless of how old or new the system is.
- Computers are newer technology than pencils but people still find pencils to be the more appropriate technology for some tasks. The same is true of paper money.

What are the details of the HCPB process?

1. Creating the ballots
   - Can be preprinted and delivered to the polling place.
   - Can be printed as a blank ballot at the polling place.

2. Storing the ballots

- In a public ballot box, of clear, see through plastic, accessible only for inserting ballots, until the counting starts.

3. Marking the ballots

- By pen or pencil.
- By electronic printing machine.
- By disabled-assistance devices.

4. Verifying the ballots

- By the voter before casting the ballot.

5. Casting the ballots

- The ballot gets inserted into a ballot box by the voter.

6. Isolating the ballots

- The ballots are kept in a ballot box that is viewable by the public and inaccessible except to deposit ballots, until the poll officials open it to count the votes.

7. Counting the ballots

- The ballots are removed from the ballot box, shuffled randomly, and counted, with each vote announced loudly to the public.

8. Reporting the results

- The resulting tallies are posted in the polling place and reported to the central authority.

9. Transporting the ballots

- Accompanied by poll workers and possibly by other representatives of opposing political interests.

10. Archiving the ballots

- Warehoused securely in a vault until the expiration date.

What are the possible problems unique to HCPB?

- Running out of paper ballots.
- Running out of pens or pencils.
- Problems other than the above are not unique to HCPB systems.

How trustworthy are HCPB systems?

(Questions like the following might be addressed.)

- Don't HCPB reopen our elections to fraud and vote rigging?
- Don't HCPB allow voters or poll workers to deposit extra ballots?
- Don't HCPB allow voters to more easily sell their votes? (This can be done in a process called "vote chaining," here-in defined.)
- Aren't HCPB more error prone than electronic voting machines?
- Aren't HCPB inaccurate?
- Isn't chain of custody a serious problem with HCPB?
- Who would select the people that do the hand-counting?
- What criteria would be used to select the hand-counters?
- How would the hand-counters be selected?
- Why do you think HCPB will produce a totally accurate result?
- Would audits ever be needed after an initial HCPB count?
- How should HCBP audits be conducted?
- How can we trust the people doing the hand-counting?
- Can't all our concerns about possible malfunctions and/or rigging of voting machines be allayed by one or more of the following?
- "Open source" software?
- The paper record of the voter's choices which is produced by some electronic voting machines? (This paper record is also sometimes called, "Voter Verified Paper Audit Trail" (VVPAT), "Voter Verified

Audit Trail" (VVAT) and "Voter Verified Paper Ballot" (VVPB). (This term is a misnomer. Since this paper record is not physically used for the official count, it's by definition not a ballot.)

- Random audits of the paper record?
- Other statistical techniques for detecting errors?
- Paper Ballots, machine counted?
- Encryption of the computerized ballots?
- Wouldn't the Holt Bill resolve all concerns about electronic voting machines?

How accessible are HCPB systems? (HAVA compliance)

- Will HCPB be a help or a hindrance to voters whose right to vote has at times been violated and suppressed—for instance, people of color, low-income people, college students?
- Will HCPB result in long lines at the polls?

How practical are HCPB?

- Aren't HCPB less accurate than electronic voting machines?
- Aren't HCPB easier to "misplace" or "damage" than the paper trail printed by touch-screen voting machines?
- Don't HCPB cost more than electronic voting machines?
- Don't some jurisdictions have ballots that are too complicated for HCPB?
- Won't HCPB create a need for additional poll workers?
- Won't HCPB demand too much time and effort from already tired poll workers?
- Won't HCPB take too much time?
- Are there "abbreviated" or "partial" versions of HCPB?
- Won't HCPB require more poll workers?

- Will it be difficult to recruit more poll workers?
- Won't HCPB require poll officials to be more highly trained than if they are using an electronic voting machine?
- Won't HCPB require poll officials to be more alert and observant than if they are using an electronic voting machine?

What can I do to get HCPB adopted in my state and my locale?

- How do I find out whether a HCPB procedure is approved in my State?
- How do I find out whether a HCPB procedure is actually used anywhere in my State?
- How do I persuade our State and/or local officials to adopt HCPB?

Other Voting Systems

Why not vote by mail, like Oregon?

- Ballots may get lost in the mail.
- Ballots may be altered or discarded by any number of people who handle the ballots before they get counted.

Why not vote via the Internet?

- Ballots can easily be hacked, either on the voting machine itself, or in transit to the central collection point.
- The receiving website may be hacked.
- Internet service may be disrupted, intentionally or unintentionally.

Why not continue to use lever machines?

- They can be hacked without being noticed.
- Like computers, they can break down.

- They are bulky and expensive to store, transport, and maintain.

Why not use punch card ballots?

- Their data is not verifiable by the voter.
- Punching the holes is an unreliable process.
- Counting is done by machines—mistakes can go unnoticed.

Aren't electronic voting machines designed to be secure?

- Manufacturers and testing companies don't allow security experts to assess the strength of the security built into the voting machines.
- Software experts have demonstrated the hackability of various systems, even without having full knowledge of those systems.
- Complicated security procedures are sometimes skipped by poll workers.
- Votes and programs are stored on credit-card-sized computer memories that are easily misplaced or substituted.
- Electronic voting systems can easily be damaged or otherwise rendered inoperable.

Why should we be concerned about electronic voting?

- The contents of the machine, and how the machine processes the ballots, is kept a secret from the public. Consequently, election outcomes are susceptible to being changed by undetectable errors, accidental or otherwise.
- The machines have a history of hardware and software breakdowns during actual elections.

Shouldn't certification of electronic voting machines remove concern?

Ideally, yes. But in practice:

- Certification is often little more than "rubber-stamp approval," based mostly on vendor assurances that problems will be fixed in the future.

- Machines are always susceptible to bugs, breakdowns, and other malfunctions.

Aren't electronic voting machines more reliable than other voting systems?

HCPB are relied upon to confirm results of other voting systems, including electronic voting machines. That means HCPB are considered more reliable than other voting systems, including electronic voting systems.

Isn't "chain of custody" easier to observe with voting machines than with HCPB?

HCPB has the clearest and most reliable chain of custody between the time the ballot is cast and the time the ballot's votes are tallied.

Isn't an electronic voting machine safe if it's not connected to another computer?

Electronic voting machines can be hacked by anyone who has access to the machine. That person does not need to be knowledgeable; hacking can be accomplished by simply inserting and then removing a memory card. This can take less than one minute.

Won't all the problems with electronic voting machines eventually be fixed?

- Systems that currently have serious problems should not in be use in critical situations. Such systems are considered by technical specialists to be in the "test" or "shakeout" phase.
- Computer experts say that all major computer software has undetected bugs-undetected and unsuspected even by the developers who created the software.
- Some computer experts promise that all such problems will be fixed some day, but their proposals are merely speculative. No foolproof strategy for protecting against all bugs and hacks has yet been put forth, and most computer experts are inclined to believe that no such strategy is possible.

Do HCPB advocates totally rule out the use of electronic voting machines?

HCPB advocates are opposed to the use of electronic voting machines in our elections, for the storing and counting of votes.

The original version of this article appeared in Scoop Independent News, 14 May, 2007 (http://www.scoop.co.nz/stories/HL0705/S00261.htm). This updated version was written solely by Sheila Parks, 16 July, 2012.

XII

On-Site Observations of the Hand-Counting of Paper Ballots and Recommendations for the General Election of 2008

Introduction

Between May 2, 2006 and November 7, 2006, I observed the hand-counting of paper ballots in three elections in two New England states. The purpose of these observations was to gather first-hand data concerning the feasibility, effectiveness and accuracy of the use of HCPB. These elections were as follows:

1. Rockport, Massachusetts (MA), on May 2, 2006, Town Election

2. Hudson, MA, on May 8, 2006, Town Election

3. Acton, Maine (ME), on November 7, 2006, General Election

All three hand-countings of paper ballots were conducted smoothly and were finished in a timely manner. This paper describes the various protocols used and presents recommendations for the use of hand-counted paper ballots (HCPB) in the upcoming elections of 2008. Absentee ballots, provisional ballots and chain of custody of the ballots are not dealt with in this paper, although they are also crucial elements of an HCPB system.[1]

Much has been written about the fraud and error associated with the use of electronic voting machines—both Direct Recording Electronic (DRE'S/touchscreens) and Optical Scan (op scans/opti scans).[2] Because of this fraud and error, HCPB have been put forth as an alternative to electronic voting machines.[3]

The use of an HCPB system will ensure that each vote is counted as intended and as cast by the voter. Although HCPB do not address the egregious suppression of the vote (mostly of people of color, elders and low income people), partnering a solution to the elimination of this suppression with the use of HCPB is the only way to have honest and transparent elections.

The jurisdictions that I observed were not selected randomly. They were places that I could drive to comfortably from my home in Boston, MA. Moreover, I was interested in observing an election in Acton, ME because the Town Clerk had told me that after the first hand-counting, the ballots would be hand-counted a second time.[4] I received permission to observe the elections from each Secretary of State, or their assistants, and from each Town Clerk. For full transparency, I introduced myself as an advocate of HCPB, who wanted to observe an HCPB election. I was very well received and felt comfortable in all places. All three Town Clerks were very generous with their time and expertise.

In each of the three elections observed, number two pencils were used by the voters to hand mark their paper ballots. In each of the elections, the counters worked in teams of two. In addition, the counters were told that it was the intent of the voter that was to be counted, and when in doubt, the counters called over the Town Clerk or Warden[5] to ask questions about specific ballots and how to count them. Finally, in each of the elections, the counters were able to hand-count the paper ballots in a short time (see specifics below).

Acton, ME, November 7, 2006, General Election

I will first describe the HCPB election in Acton, ME on November 7, 2006 because this protocol used a procedure that would produce the most accurate count of the votes—namely, a second hand-count was done immediately after the first hand-count.

The ballot box was a plain, wooden box with a slot into which voters put their ballots. There were six teams, of two counters each, doing the hand-counting. The counters came in specifically to count; they had not worked at the polls earlier in the day. Each team consisted of a Republican and a Democrat. The teams first counted the ballots into batches of 50, and then these batches of 50 were counted again.

The teams then hand-counted the votes cast in each contest for each batch of 50 ballots in the following manner: one member of the team would read out loud the name marked off for each contest; the other member of the team marked the vote on a tally sheet that corresponded to the ballot. A voter's entire ballot was tallied for all of the contests before the counters went on to tally the next voter's ballot. The talliers counted each vote by making a hash mark (small, straight vertical line).[6] After four vertical lines were made, a fifth line was made diagonally through the first four marks. For each person running for office (and for each initiative), the tally sheet was marked off into five columns vertically and two rows horizontally, providing 10 rectangular spaces in each of which five hash marks could be written—a total of 50 hash marks—i.e., votes per contest or initiative. A dark horizontal line separated the names in each contest. At the end of the counting of all of the races in a batch of 50 ballots, the counters totaled the hash marks for each race on the tally sheet and entered that number on the tally sheet in the "TOTAL VOTE" column. There was a special sheet for write-ins.

Immediately after the first hand-count of a batch of 50 ballots, a second hand-count, on a new tally sheet, was done of this same batch of 50 ballots by these same counters. Again, the entire ballot of each voter was tallied before the counters proceeded to the next voter's ballot. This time, the person who had read the names out loud marked each vote on the tally sheet, and the person who had tallied read out loud the ballot choices. After the votes on all 50 ballots in a batch were marked on the tally sheet, the totals for each contest were obtained and written on the tally sheet. If the totals for the candidates in any contest or for any initiative were not exactly the same on the first and second tally sheets (i.e. on the first and second countings), these contests or initiatives were counted a third time. I observed such a situation two times.

The HCPB election in Acton, ME demonstrates that paper ballots can be hand-counted immediately a second time, at the precinct on election night, before the results are posted at the precinct, in order to ensure an honest and transparent count in a timely manner. The election in Acton, ME also indicates that paper ballots can be hand-counted in a very short time. With seven races and two initiatives, the six teams of two people each were able to hand-count twice 944 ballots in four hours.

Rockport, MA, May 2, 2006, Town Election, Hudson, MA, May 8, 2006, Town Election

The elections in Rockport and Hudson will be discussed together because they were similar in various respects. Both counted the votes cast only once,[7] and both used the same kind of tally sheets provided by the MA Secretary of State. In both jurisdictions the ballots were counted into batches of 50. The tally sheet was a large piece of paper that was marked off into a grid with horizontal and vertical lines forming small rectangular boxes (similar to the squares of graph paper). The vertical columns were marked with a heavy line at each multiple of five columns. There were 50 rectangular boxes across each horizontal line. At the top of the tally sheet, each vertical column was numbered from 1-50. On both the left hand and right hand sides of the tally sheet were the names of the people running in that particular race. One tally, as a hash mark, was put into one box, beside the name of the person voted for. A voter's entire ballot was tallied for all of the contests before the counters went on to tally the next voter's ballot. After the 50 ballots were tallied, the totals for each contest were entered into the "Totals" column at the end of the 50th box. Blanks and write-ins were also marked on this sheet. Four or five teams of two poll workers did the hand-count. One read from the ballot, and the other person placed the hash mark in the appropriate box on the tally sheet.

Rockport, MA used an old wooden ballot box.[8] A poll worker turned the brass handle on the box as each voter put her/his ballot into the box. Numbers on the front of the box automatically changed as ballots were placed in it, counting the cumulative number of ballots placed in the box. The ballot box marked each ballot with the precinct number down the center of the ballot as it went through. The preceding characteristics of the ballot box provided a measure of security for the ballots, minimizing the danger of stuffing the ballot box, a criticism often leveled at the HCPB process. As noted earlier, this paper does not examine in detail issues of security such as chain of custody, but rather deals with protocols for HCPB.

There were two crews of poll workers, morning and afternoon. One crew came in at 6:30 AM and worked until 12:30 PM. The second crew came in at 12:30 PM and worked until 6:30 PM. At 6:30 PM, the second crew went home for dinner until 8 PM, when they came back to hand-count the paper ballots. The morning shift came back at 6:30 PM to work at the polls and then to hand-count the paper ballots. The polls closed at 8 PM. The paper ballots were hand-counted by five teams of two workers each.

In Hudson, the ballot box was an old box made of gray wood. The ballot box rang when the voter put in her/his ballot, and the poll worker turned the crank of the box, moving the ballot from the slot of the box into the box. When the poll worker cranked the ballot into the ballot box, each ballot was inked with "Town of Hudson, precinct 6."[9] This ballot box also provided a degree of security for the ballots.

The Clerk could hire eight people per precinct, not including the Warden and Clerk, who were also present for the hand-counting. There were two shifts of poll workers, 7 AM to 5 PM and 5 PM to 8 PM, which was when the polls closed. The second shift did the counting. Poll workers had to be registered voters in the town of Hudson. Although it was preferred that the counters lived in the precinct where they worked, it was not necessary.

The elections in Rockport and Hudson again demonstrate that paper ballots can be hand-counted in a reasonable time. In Rockport, it took about one hour to hand-count 522 ballots; there were six races and no initiatives. In Hudson it took about one hour to hand-count 59 ballots; there were 14 races and no initiatives. As noted, both communities used ballot boxes that provided a degree of security for the ballots.

Recommendations To Begin With The 2008 General Election (Which Includes The Presidential Election)

Recommendations Based on My Observations
1. Based on my observations in Acton, ME, this paper recommends the hand-counting of paper ballots followed immediately by a complete second hand-counting and a reconciliation of the two counts, if necessary, by additional counting.[10] A second hand-counting is crucial to check the accuracy of the first hand-count. If a discrepancy is found between the two countings, counting should continue until the counts are reconciled. This paper also recommends the procedure used in Acton of counting the ballots into batches of 50, counting a batch of 50 and then immediately counting that batch of 50 again. Some critics of electronic voting machines have pointed out the need to obtain a second count, called an audit, after the first original tabulation of votes; however, there is no consensus as to how such an audit should or could be done. The second counting of ballots recommended in this paper goes beyond the concept of an audit to a comprehensive process encompassing a second counting of every vote and a reconciliation of the two counts.
2. From my observations of these three hand countings, I prefer the tally sheets used in Acton, ME over the graph-like grid used in both Rockport, MA and Hudson, MA. During my observations, it appeared that the Acton tally sheet was easier for the counters to use. With the grid-like tally sheets, care had to be taken by the counters not to lose their place.
3. Because HCPB require careful attention to and scrutiny of the ballots, it is recommended that people who have not worked at the polls all day come in to do the counting, as in Acton, ME.

As noted, this paper does not deal in detail with the issue of security of the ballots. However, it is recommended that research be done concerning the cost of manufacturing ballot boxes with the characteristics described for Hudson, MA and Rockport, MA.

Additional Recommendations

I have been involved with voting rights since the 2000 presidential election and the fiasco in Florida. Based on my previous work,[11] I include the following, expanded HCPB recommendations:

1. In addition to the four recommendations presented above, it is recommended that an HCPB protocol also have the following characteristics:

    a. Ballots would be counted at the precinct by registered voters in that precinct.
    b. The counting would be done in full view of the public.
    c. The counting would be videotaped.
    d. The results would be posted at the precinct immediately after the count.
    e. To be manageable, precincts would be no larger than 1000 registered voters. (Because the concept of HCPB operates at the precinct level, even large communities can adopt such a system.)
    f. In each precinct there would be at least 10 teams of two counters each (a Democrat and a Republican).[12] These teams would count the ballots, one counter reading the name and the other counter making the mark on the tally sheet. For the second counting, the counters on each team would switch roles.
    g. Whether or not there would be observers as part of the team of counters, and if so, how many, needs more research and is beyond the scope of this paper.

2. This paper recommends that poll workers who participate in the process of HCPB be paid at a rate that will be respected by the community. This will be possible because a large amount of money will be saved with the elimination of electronic voting machines. The Help America Vote Act (HAVA) paid states hundreds of millions of dollars to buy electronic voting machines, both DRE'S and/or op scans.[13] One machine can cost anywhere from $3,000 and $5,000[14] and that amount does not include storing, maintenance, and upgrade. In contrast, for an HCPB election, the cost for the counting could be $2400.00 per precinct for each election, with ten teams of two workers each, as described above, and paying each worker $20/hour for six hours ($120). HCPB by registered voters from the precinct would also keep the money in the community. As is true

for op scan electronic voting machines, money would also have to be spent for the cost of printing the ballots.[15] If hundreds of millions of dollars had not been spent for the purchase, storage and upgrade of electronic voting machines, imagine the money our communities could have used for health care and education.

Epilogue

On January 4, 2006, I had the good fortune to watch on TV the voting in Congress for Speaker of the House. One at a time, each representative called out orally her/his choice for Speaker, and that vote was tallied by hand. This hand counting of oral votes was done by two Republicans and two Democrats, all of whom had been appointed by the Clerk of the House. The Electronic Board that usually counts the votes of the Representatives was not used for this count; the official vote was tallied by hand. I could not help but wonder how the Representatives would have felt had their votes not been recorded accurately, or not at all, as voters throughout the USA experienced in recent elections. For voters in each precinct in the USA, hand-counting of paper ballots would assure that each of our votes is counted as intended and as cast, as the oral votes of our Representatives, were hand-counted, as intended and as cast, in the House of Representatives.

This article originally appeared in OpEdNews, 18 July, 2007 (http://www.opednews.com/articles/opedne_sheila_p_070718_on_site_observations.htm).

Endnotes

[1] For a beginning discussion of chain of custody, see *"Chapter III—Hand-Counted Paper Ballots Now."* "Ballot boxes must be clearly marked and visible in plain view. Ballot boxes will be sealed and locked whenever they contain ballots and are not being actively used. Ballot boxes are secured from the beginning of voting until the end of counting by a chain of custody procedure. Ballot boxes never leave the polling place until after the vote is counted, audited and certified. Each time ballot boxes move from the physical control of or visual contact from one person to another, a duplicate record signed by all counters and observers must be made relinquishing and gaining control. There will be a documentation process wherein each ballot box will have a record of its handling from the beginning of the day to the end of counting. On the web site of computer science expert Professor Douglas W. Jones, there is a very clear and detailed protocol for "Ballot and Ballot Box Transportation" and "Ballot Storage." The reader is referred specifically to these two sections (the last two on this link): http://www.cs.uiowa.edu/~jones/voting/paper.html.

[2] Listed here are some of the outstanding articles about the fraud and error resulting from electronic voting machines; some are from the mainstream media, others from scholarly sources, and yet others from technical groups:

The public hacking of electronic voting machines, by Hari Hursti working with Blackboxvoting.org, 21 February, 2007 <http://www.bbvforums.org/forums/messages/2197/6847.html>.

"September 2005 Report on Elections" U.S. Government Accountability Office (GAO) in its nonpartisan report states in its conclusions: "Numerous recent studies and reports have highlighted problems with the security and reliability of electronic voting systems…the concerns they raise have the potential to affect election outcomes…Federal Efforts to Improve Security and Reliability of Electronic Voting Systems Are Under Way, But Key Activities Need to be Completed," 07 March, 2007 <http://www.gao.gov/new.items/d05956.pdf>.

Robert F. Kennedy, Jr., "Will the Next Election be Hacked?" <u>Rolling Stone Magazine</u>, # 1002, 15 June, 2006 <http://www.rollingstone.com/politics/story/11717105/robert_f_kennedy_jr__will_the_next_election_be_hacked/>. Note: retrieved from the web 07 July, 2012; to view this article, you must be a print subscriber and registered for online access at http://www.rollingstone.com/allaccess/search. A similar article by Kennedy, "The 2004 Presidential election was stolen via institutional fraud," is available at<http://wisconsinwave.org/news/robert-f-kennedy-jr-2004-presidential-election-was-stolen-institutional-fraud>.

"Report of the Brennan Center Task Force of NYU," 27 June, 2006 <http://www.brennancenter.org/press_detail.asp?key=100&subkey=36345> and 22 February, 2007 <http://brennancenter.org/dynamic/subpages/download_file_38150.pdf>. Note: this second link produced an error on the web on 07 July, 2012.

Ed Felten *et al.*, "Security Analysis of the Diebold AccuVote-TS Voting Machine," Princeton Center for Information Technology, Princeton University, Sept. 2006.

<http://citpsite.s3-website-us-east-1.amazonaws.com/oldsite-htdocs/voting/>.

Rachel Kapochunas, "Jennings Officially Contests Race in Florida's 13th District," The New York Times, 20 February, 2007; Problems that occurred with electronic voting machines in many states in the General Election on November 7, 2006, especially the 18,000 under-votes in Sarasota County, FL. <http://www.nytimes.com/cq/2006/12/20/cq_2056.html>.

National Institute of Standards and Technology, discussion draft, 01 December, 2006 <http://vote.nist.govDraftWhitePaperOnSIinVVSG2007-20061120.pdf>. Note: this link could not produce any results from the web 07 July, 2012.

Rady Ananda, "The annotated bibliography," 11 May, 2007 <http://tinyurl.com/2gwlve>.

[3] Listed here are examples of the outstanding work people and groups have done to put forth ways to have ballots be hand-counted, so as to do away with the fraud and error of the electronic voting machines:

Nancy Tobi, "The Granite State Delivers Rock-Solid Information on Hand Counting," 04 August, 2006 <http://www.opednews.com/articles/genera_nancy_to_060804_the_granite_state_de.htm>.

An editorial first carried in the Ketchikan Daily News, 01 December, 2006, Ed. Terry Miller, called for HCPB for the president and vice president, <http://www.ketchikandailynews.com>. (Thanks to John Gideon of The Voting News for pointing out the Ketchikan editorial.) On 07 December, 2006, the editorial was then picked up by the Juneau Empire <http://juneauempire.com>. (Neither of these documents were available on the internet, 08 July, 2012.)

Rady Ananda wrote an "HCPB Implementation Strategy for 2007," 03 January, 2007 <http://www.opednews.com/articles/opedne_rady_ana_070102_evoting_exit_strateg.htm>.

In February 2007, Phil Lindsey, introduced an initiative to go on the ballot that, if passed, would mean that MO would not use electronic voting machines in their elections, but would use HCPB. This initiative must first get enough votes from the public to appear on the ballot; Michael Collins, "Missouri Activists Say 'Show Me The Vote,'" Scoop Independent News <http://www.scoop.co.nz/stories/HL0702/S00271.htm>.

Another former HCPB initiative, led by Kathleen Wynne, was in the form of a petition from the American People to Congress, urging Congress to reintroduce the Paper Ballot Bill of 2006.

In June 2007, at The DFA (Democracy for America) Democracy Fest in New Hampshire, in a telephone call to the attendees, Representative Dennis Kucinich stated that he will introduce The Paper Ballot Bill of 2007, mandating HCPB for all federal offices. Kucinich has changed the bill from his 2006 version, H.R. 6200, which had mandated HCPB for the offices of president and vice-president only <http://frwebgate.access.gpo.gov/cgi-bin/getdoc.cgi?dbname=109_cong_bills&docid=f:h6200ih.txt.pdf>, retrieved from the web, March 30, 2007. This link could not be found on the internet,

09 August, 2012. The following is a shortened link: <http://www.govtrack.us/congress/bills/109/hr6200>. Retrieved from the web, 09 August, 2012.

[4] I observed one of the three HCPB methods authorized by the Maine Secretary of State, called 'The Reading Method.' "The team counts each lot together; 1 member reads and the other member tallies. The team members then switch roles, so that the tally is done a second time. If they agree, that count is completed. If there is a discrepancy, the team must recount the race or races where the count was off...." Maine Revised Statutes Annotated (MRSA), "Conduct Of Elections," Ch. 9, p. 3, (Title 21-A §695). A link could not be found on the internet to these statutes, 15 July, 2012.

[5] "Warden" is the name used in Massachusetts for the poll worker in charge of the election in that precinct. Different names are used in different states. The person is not an elected official.

[6] In April 2004, Teresa Hommel described some hand-counting methods used in Canada and New York City; "How to Hand-count Votes Marked on Paper Ballots," WheresThePaper.org <http://wheresthepaper.org/CountPaperBallots.htm>.

[7] Another method of hand-counting paper ballots is the sort and stack protocol, <http://sos.nh.gov/search.aspx?searchtext=sort%20and%20stack> This link takes you to the election procedure manual (EPM) 04 October, 2011. Pages 149-152 describe the sort and stack method (Section XXVI, "Hand-counting Instructions-Model 1, Sort and Stack by Candidate Method). In this method, used by the state of New Hampshire, the ballots are first sorted into stacks for each candidate, and then the stacks are counted. In e-mail correspondence, December 2, 2006 and December 4, 2006, with Nancy Tobi from Democracy for New Hampshire, Tobi states that NH uses the sort and stack method for both election night counts and for recounts. She says that it is used primarily for "… single member races—where there is a yes/no choice…." and for straight ticket votes. Sort and stack is not usable in all situations. With this protocol, as with those used in Rockport and Hudson, votes are counted only once; the manual recommends a second count if there is a "close race." A "close race" is not defined. A mandatory second count for all ballots could be added to this protocol.

[8] The ballot box said "Town of Rockport, Precinct 2," and was dated 1922.

[9] The ballot box was made by S. Ralph Cross and Sons, Inc., 120 Mayfield Street, Worcester 2, MA, now out of business. The box was dated 1971.

[10] Joanne Karasak has recommended a first count followed by "an immediate second 'blind' count' (blind count meaning that the second team of counters do not know the total on the first count)." E-mail posted June 26, 2007. Based on my observations in Maine, I think it would be too confusing to change counters.

[11] See *"Chapter II: What Went Wrong in Ohio and Black Box Voting," "Chapter III: Hand-Counted Paper Ballots Now"* (see endnote 1); and *"Chapter XI: Hand-Counted Paper Ballots: Frequently Asked Questions."*

[12] If there are additional parties on the ballot, representatives from these parties should also participate in the counting.

[13] "Help America Vote Act Of 2002," 107th Congress Public Law 252. U.S. Government Printing Office Thanks to my good friend Lucius Chiaraviglio, HCPB activist, for his help with this endnote <http://frwebgate.access.gpo.gov/cgi-bin/getdoc.cgi?dbname=107_cong_public_laws&docid=f:publ252.107>.

[14] Thanks to my good friend Paul Lehto for sending me this information. "Agreement Between Snohomish County, Washington and the Sequoia Voting Systems, Inc. for the Purchase of the AVC Edge Electronic Voting System," Appendix A, 27, March, 2007 <http://www.votersunite.org/info/SequoiaContract.pdf> for a detailed example of what electronic voting machines cost. This contract was for more than five million dollars. Appendix A is contained in his lawsuit against Sequoia Voting Systems, Inc., 18 March, 2007 <http://www.votersunite.org/info/lehtolawsuit.asp>.

[15] E-mail correspondence, 06 March, 2007, with Chief Legal Counsel, Election Division, Office of the Secretary of State, MA. In MA in 2006 there were 71 precincts using HCPB. For the MA State Primary election in 2006, the cost was $444 per precinct (which included two parties) for ballot printing, which included absentee ballots, specimen ballots and instruction cards. For the General Election in 2006, the cost was $391 per precinct.

XIII

Sort and Stack Elections in New Hampshire

Introduction

In July of 2007, I published a paper titled "*On-Site Observations of the Hand-Counting of Paper Ballots and Recommendations for the General Election of 2008.*"[1] In this paper, I described on-site observations of the hand-counting of paper ballots in three elections in two New England States: Rockport and Hudson, MA and Acton, ME. All of these hand-counted paper ballots (HCPB) elections used the read and tally[2] protocol for counting the ballots. With this protocol, teams of two counters are used: one counter reads out loud the name the voter has marked for each contest (or each initiative), and the other member of the team records the vote on a tally sheet that corresponds to the ballot. (For a fuller description of the read and tally HCPB protocol, see "*Chapter XII: On-Site Observations of the Hand-Counting of Paper Ballots and Recommendations for the General Election of 2008.*") The procedure I liked the most was that used by Acton, ME, in which the ballots were counted twice.

During the period of observation of the HCPB elections in Rockport and Hudson, MA and Acton, ME between May 2, 2006 and November 7, 2006, I did not observe a HCPB method called sort and stack, which is used in New Hampshire (NH). I wanted to observe some sort and stack elections in order to have more complete knowledge of the methods used for HCPB.

I called the NH Secretary of State's Election Division to find out which municipalities in NH use the sort and stack protocol. The woman I spoke with in the Election Division suggested that I call the individual municipalities to find out which ones use sort and stack to hand-count ballots.

New Hampshire Municipalities that use Sort and Stack

The website of the NH Secretary of State, Election Division, lists the names of all the cities and towns in NH as well as the names of the city and town clerks.[3] The website also gives the names of all the municipalities that use AccuVote optical scan machines for voting.[4] From these two lists, I derived the names of the cities and towns that do not use AccuVote optical scan machines and therefore use HCPB.

There were 236 municipalities on Secretary of State William Gardner's list of city and town clerks. AccuVote electronic voting machines were used by 108 municipalities. That left 128 municipalities that use HCPB. That number was not completely up-to-date, as three places had changed or were going to change over to electronic voting machines.[5] That left 125 municipalities that do not use electronic voting machines but rather HCPB. I spoke with 123 of these municipalities.[6] I did not reach Ellsworth, whose population in 2000 was 87 or Windsor, whose population in 2005 was 237. Since these were very small municipalities, it did not seem to me to be crucial for this paper which HCPB methodology they used.

In most cases, I spoke directly with the Town Clerk. In a few cases I spoke with an assistant to the Town Clerk and in some, to the Town Moderator of the municipality. The moderators run the elections in NH. I said that I was an HCPB advocate, doing research on HCPB protocols. The questions I asked each city or town were: How many registered voters are there in your municipality and what method of HCPB do you use. I then asked them to explain the method to me.[7] The people I spoke with were helpful, friendly and forthcoming. From my conversations, I learned that of the 123 municipalities in NH with which I spoke that use HCPB, 114 use the read and tally protocol (called the ballot-by-ballot method in the Manual of the NH Secretary of State), while only nine use the sort and stack protocol, although not entirely.

The following is a list of the nine NH municipalities using the sort and stack method. The first four use sort and stack in some circumstances, and read and tally in other circumstances. The last five municipalities use sort and stack exclusively.

1. Andover: Number of registered voters—1,615. Uses sort and stack and also read and tally, depending on how many candidates are on the ballot. Does not have a specific rule for when read and tally or sort and stack is used, except that if there are only two candidates, the sort and stack method is used.
2. Greenfield: Number of registered voters—1,000+. In an uncontested town election, sort and stack is used.[8] Generally read and tally is used.
3. Greenville: Number of registered voters—1,200. Uses sort and stack only if there is one yes/no question on the ballot. If in a zoning election, e.g., there were 6-7 questions that were yes/no, would do read and tally. Uses read and tally if there are two or more contestants,

including presidential races.
4. Hinsdale: Number of registered voters—2,405. Uses sort and stack and read and tally. Counters decide which method they use.
5. Langdon: Number of registered voters—447.
6. Marlborough: Number of registered voters—1,522.
7. Orford: Number of registered voters—800 or 900.
8. Plainfield: Number of registered voters—1,605.
9. Walpole: Number of registered voters—2,626.

On-site Observations of Sort and Stack Elections in New Hampshire

Because Walpole had the largest number of registered voters (2,626), and uses sort and stack exclusively, I asked Ernie Vose, Town Moderator, if it would be possible to observe the sort and stack counting of ballots in Walpole.[9] He graciously agreed. On January 8, 2008, I observed the hand-counting of ballots for the US presidential primary election in Walpole. There were 22 candidates on the Democratic ballot, and 21 candidates on the Republican ballot. The total number of ballots counted was 1,786: Democrats 1,057 and Republicans 729. On March 11, 2008, I observed the hand-counting of the Town Meeting election in Walpole. The total number of ballots counted was 625.

Most of the hand-counters came in to count when the polls closed and had not been there all day. There is a polling place in North Walpole, and these ballots are brought to Walpole to be counted, together with the rest of the ballots from Walpole.

In the primary election, there were eleven teams of two people counting the ballots. In the Town Meeting election, there were 13 teams of two counters counting the ballots. Each team of counters sat at a separate table. There were no official observers watching the counters at any of the tables. The Town Moderator paired the counters. He described the process as follows: "We pair the counters by a 'veteran' and a new person if needed. We do not consider party affiliation. Many are undeclared. People cannot count if they are on the ballot."[10]

After all the ballots were taken from the ballot boxes, they were counted into batches of 25. These batches of 25 ballots were put crisscross to make a pile of 100 ballots. The ballots were then distributed to the tables. For the Town Meeting election, there were different color coded ballots, and some of the ballots were more complicated than others. The more complicated the ballot, the less ballots for a table. The less complicated the ballot, the more ballots for a table. The Town Moderator distributed the ballots accordingly. Each counter at the table took half of the total ballots at that table.

Sort and stack is done silently. The ballots are sorted into stacks by the counters, according to the candidate or question/warrant article (yes/no) being voted for. There are also stacks for under-votes, over-votes and write-ins. This is the first time that a pair of eyes sees the vote (and makes sure it goes into the right stack). Then the votes are counted, both by hand and by the eyes of the counter at the same time as counting. That is, not only does the counter manually count the stack of ballots, but also the counter looks at each name (or yes/no of a question) as she or he counts. This is the second time a pair of eyes sees the vote. After the votes are counted and the number recorded, the counters switch stacks and the votes are counted again both by eyes and by hand. This is the third time a pair of eyes sees the vote.[11]

The counters did not look at the number of total votes for each candidate or question that the other counter had recorded. When both counters were finished counting the votes for a candidate or question, they then compared the totals they had written for each candidate or question. If there was a discrepancy, both people counted again. The two counters did not observe each other counting; each counter counted her/his own stack at the same time that the other counter did. The counters counted so fast, as they went from ballot to ballot, that I could not see the names or yes/no on the ballots as they counted.

In the primary election, I observed only tables counting the Democratic votes; I did not observe any tables counting the Republican votes. Also, various tables did the process a little differently.[12] There were two ways the ballots were sorted and stacked and then counted:

1. The ballots were sorted and stacked for the seven Democratic candidates out of 22 who received votes so that there were seven stacks on the table at the same time, one for each of the seven candidates who received votes. There were also stacks for under-votes, over-votes and write-ins. Then each stack was counted, as described above.
2. The ballots were sorted and stacked separately for each of the seven Democratic primary candidates who received votes from the 22 running and for under-votes, over-votes and write-ins—that is, the ballots were sorted and stacked and then counted seven different times, once for each candidate who received votes. As ballots were sorted, a stack was made for each candidate. Then each stack was counted. After each sort and stack and count, the ballots were put together again and then sorted, stacked and counted for another candidate.

Discussion of Sort and Stack Method

In NH, more than half of the municipalities count ballots by hand—at least 123 of the total 236 municipalities. However, the use of sort and stack surprisingly is not widespread in NH, with only nine municipalities using this method. Of these nine, only five use sort and stack exclusively, while four use sort and stack under certain circumstances, but prefer read and tally in other circumstances.

In a talk given by NH Assistant Secretary of State Anthony Stevens at Democracy Fest in NH, on June 10, 2007 titled "Hand Counting Paper Ballots," Stevens stated that the "Secretary of State [of NH] indicates a preferred method [of hand-counting paper ballots] in [the] NH Election Procedure Manual."[13] This manual is presented on the website of the NH Secretary of State.[14] In the manual, sort and stack is described as follows: "This model [sort and stack] is presented as a best practice in hand counting, based on the secretary of state's experience with hand recounts."[15] Thus, Gardner's preference is based on hand recounts and not necessarily with sort and stack as the HCPB method of counting votes on election night. The NH Manual further states: "…This ballot sort and stack method is considered the faster and easier method, even though each mark is seen more times than the method using ballot reading and tally marks. Counters who have tried other methods express more pleasure with the sort and stack method because (a) it is simpler to count, and (b) counters are more confident in the results."[16]

In his talk, Stevens also said that the "Sort-and-stack method may not be used widely in New Hampshire on election night."[17] That indeed turned out to be the case, as only nine municipalities use sort and stack in any elections. In several telephone conversations with me, Stevens was very helpful. On August 26, 2008, he noted that he prefers the sort and stack method on election night; however, he stated that he would not and could not push the sort and stack method on any municipality.[18] In NH, each Town Moderator, by law, chooses the way votes are counted.[19] In our conversation, Stevens further said that he is currently reaching out to municipalities in NH to teach the sort and stack method. It will be interesting to see if Stevens is successful in teaching the sort and stack method and getting a larger number of municipalities to adopt it. The small number of municipalities using sort and stack was surprising, given the strong endorsement by the Secretary of State and Assistant Secretary of State of NH.

Sort and stack worked well in Walpole, NH. Ernie Vose, the Town Moderator, was very skilled and effective in the implementation of this method. As far as I know, he is the only Town Moderator in NH who uses sort and stack in all elections, even ones in which there are multiple seat races. It is important to note that the NH Manual states that the Secretary of State's preference for sort and stack is "based on the secretary of state's experience *with hand recounts* [emphasis mine]."[20] Therefore, Gardner could be extrapolating from less complicated recounts to elections that could be more complicated.

Both sort and stack elections that I observed in Walpole were done efficiently and finished in a timely manner. Vose noted that it takes a lot of time after the counting to record the data into the computers.[21] The effectiveness of the sort and stack method in Walpole makes it potentially a model that could be followed by other municipalities in NH and across the country if they so wished—at least in simple elections.

This paper has described the sort and stack method of HCPB used in NH, while a previous paper described the read and tally method used in ME and MA. As noted in the present paper, the NH Secretary of State and Assistant Secretary of State prefer sort and stack, but most municipalities using HCPB use read and tally. Only 9 of 123 municipalities use sort and stack, and not in all circumstances. What can be said about the two methods?[22]

There are certain differences between the two. First, in the read and tally method, there is a written record of each individual vote cast, as well as the total number of votes each candidate or question received.[23] In the sort and stack method, there is only a total vote count for each candidate or initiative on the tally sheet—no written record of each vote that was counted. On the other hand, with sort and stack the ballots are always counted twice (once by each counter) and this is not necessarily so with read and tally. In the three read and tally elections I observed, only one used an HCPB protocol that hand-counted the ballots twice. Second, as noted earlier, the NH Manual states that sort and stack is faster than read and tally.[24] However, sort and stack, while fast, may sometimes be too fast in some instances. In the sort and stack elections that I observed, the counting of the stacks was done so rapidly that there was no way for me as an unofficial observer to see the name or yes/no on the ballot in each stack as it was counted. In read and tally, it is possible to see the name or yes/no on each ballot as it is counted and then recorded.[25] A third difference between the two methods, is that sort and stack is done silently, so the room is quieter than with read and tally.

Beyond these differences, there are important similarities. Both sort and stack and read and tally were used efficiently in all the elections I observed. Moreover, and most significantly, in the read and tally election in Acton, ME and in both of the sort and stack elections in Walpole, NH, the ballots were counted twice. I strongly recommend that in all HCPB elections, the ballots be counted twice—the second counting immediately following the first.[26] A second counting guarantees greater accuracy and could be considered an audit. The question remains: why don't we do it right the first time—i.e., hand-count the ballots on election night? Hand-counting the ballots twice on election night (the second counting immediately after the first) would do away with the fraud and error rampant with the use of electronic voting machine counting.

Epilogue

On September 27, 2008, I was an official observer in Boston, MA in a recount for one of the two Democratic candidates in a primary contest for state senator. In this recount, the ballots were hand-counted by the read and tally method. There were eight tables, with two counters at each table. One counter read the name on the ballot, and the other counter made a tally on the tally sheet. There were four observers at each of the eight tables: two observers (one for each candidate) observed the reader of the ballot and two observers (again one for each candidate) observed the tallier. It was possible to actually observe the names on the ballot as well as each mark that was recorded on the tally sheet. At the conclusion of the recount for this highly contested race in a large urban area, both candidates accepted the results. This recount demonstrates both the manageability and accuracy of the hand-counting of paper ballots. In this recount, 11,227 ballots were counted—a very large number—with accuracy and in a relatively short time—four and one half hours. In this case, read and tally was used; the same manageability and accuracy would most likely have occurred with sort and stack.

This article originally appeared in OpEdNews, 08 October, 2008 (http://www.opednews.com/articles/sort-and-stack-elections-i-by-Sheila-Parks-081028-309.html).

Endnotes

[1] See *"Chapter XII: On-Site Observations of the Hand-counting of Paper Ballots and Recommendations for the General Election Of 2008."*

[2] The read and tally HCPB protocol is also called read and mark. The two terms seem to be used interchangeably. The web site of the Secretary of State of NH calls this method "All Offices, Ballot-By-Ballot Method." Originally <http://www.sos.state.nh.us/FINAL%20EPM%208-30-2006.pdf>, page 147, retrieved from the web January 4, 2008. (The link no longer leads to the page, 09 July, 2012.)

[3] Originally <http://www.sos.nh.gov/clerks.htm>, retrieved from the web June 6, 2008. The table I worked with is no longer on the website; it was labeled "2008 (updated July 12, 2007)". I have a hard copy of this table. There have been some changes in town clerks, but otherwise the two lists are the same.

[4] Originally <http://www.sos.nh.gov/voting%20machines2006.htm>, retrieved from the web, June 6, 2008. The table I worked with is no longer on the website; it was labeled "(as of July 2007)". I have a hard copy of this table. These two tables are the same, except for the three jurisdictions that had already changed over to machines or were going to do so, when I spoke with them. The table I used did not have these municipalities listed as using AccuVote. The new table does.

[5] Conway, East Kingston, Plymouth. As noted, these three towns are now included in the table listing the jurisdictions that use AccuVote.

[6] Acworth, Albany, Alexandria, Alstead, Andover, Antrim, Bartlett, Bath, Bennington, Benton, Bethlehem, Boscawen, Bradford, Bridgewater, Bristol, Brookfield, (Campton, which was not on SOS list for machines, used machines), Caroll, Center Harbor, Charlestown, Chatham, Chesterfield, Chichester, Clarksville, Colebrook, Columbia, Cornish, Croyden, Dalton, Danbury, Deering, Dixville, Dorchester, Dublin, Dummer, Dunbarton, (East Kingston switched to machines), Easton, Eaton, Effingham, Errol, Francestown, Franconia, Freedom, Gilsum, Goshen, Greenfield, Greenville, Groton, Hancock, Harrisville, Harts Location, Haverhill, Hebron, Hill, Hinsdale, Holderness, Jackson, Jefferson, Kensington, Lancaster, Landaff, Langdon, Lempster, Lincoln, Lisbon, Lyman, Lyme, Lyndeborough, Madbury, Marlborough, Marlow, Mason, Middeton, Millsfield, Monroe, Mont Vernon, Nelson, New Castle, Newington, Newport, Northfield, Northumberland, Orange, Orford, Piermont, Pittsburg, Plainfield, (Plymouth going to machines), Randolph, Richmond, Rollinsford, Roxbury, Rumney, Salisbury, Sandwich, Sharon, Shelburne, South Hampton, Springfield, Stark, Stewartstown, Stoddard, Strafford, Stratford, Sugar Hill, Sullivan, Surry, Sutton, Temple, Thornton, Troy, Tuftonboro, Unity, Walpole, Warner, Warren, Washington, Waterville Valley, Webster, Westmoreland, Whitefield, Wilmot, Wilton, Woodstock.

[7] I learned a lot about different nuanced ways to do a read and tally hand-count.

[8] They must use sort and stack even with only one name on the ballot, because of under-votes, over-votes and write-ins.

[9] Thanks to Nancy Tobi of Democracy for New Hampshire who strongly suggested I contact the Town Moderator of Walpole, NH about sort and stack elections.

[10] Ernie Vose, Moderator of Walpole, e-mail correspondence, January 12, 2008, in response to my question.

[11] This paragraph is a compilation of a conversation with an election official at the Walpole election on why she liked sort and stack so much, my own observations of the hand-counting at the Walpole elections, and phone conversations with Anthony Stevens, NH Assistant Secretary of State, August and September, 2008.

[12] Conversation with Ernie Vose, January 1, 2008.

[13] Originally <http://www.democracyfornewhampshire.com/files/Hand_count_training_D-fest_July_5_2007.pdf> retrieved from the web November 4, 2007. (This link could not be found on the internet, 09 July, 2012.) I was not present at his talk and saw his words on his powerpoint presentation posted on the Internet.

[14] NH Secretary of State, "The New Hampshire Election Procedure Manual 2006-2007," retrieved from the web January 4, 2008.

[15] "The New Hampshire Election Procedure Manual," 144; retrieved from the web January 4, 2008. Page 144 deals with sort and stack, called by the Manual, "Sort And Stack By Candidate Method." Page 147 deals with read and tally, called by the Manual, "All Offices, Ballot-By-Ballot Method." This manual is no longer on the internet. Please see endnote 7 in *"Chapter XII: On-Site Observations and Recommendations for 2008,"* for the most current version of The New Hampshire Election Procedure Manual, retrieved from the web 17 July, 2012. Pages 149-152 deal with sort and stack. Pages 153-156 deal with the read and tally, called by the manual, "all offices, ballot-by-ballot method."

[16] "The New Hampshire Election Procedure Manual," 144. Retrieved from the web November 4, 2007. Pages 149-152 in most current version. See endnote 15 above.

[17] Hand_count_training_D-fest_July_5_2007.pdf, retrieved from the web November 4, 2007. (This link could not be found on the internet, 09 July, 2012.)

[18] Telephone conversation with Anthony Stevens, August 26, 2008.

[19] "The New Hampshire Election Procedure Manual 2006-2007," 144, retrieved from the web, January 4, 2008. Page 144: "...State law authorizes the moderator to choose the system of hand counting to be used and to supervise the counting. RSA 659:60...However, neither state law nor the Secretary of State require that any particular system of counting be used. Moderators should ensure that that system of counting they adopt is accurate and efficient." And again, page 149: "NOTE: This is a model describing how some moderators have chosen to count ballots. State law authorizes the moderator to choose the system of hand counting to be used and to supervise the counting. RSA 659:60. This model [ballot-by-ballot] is presented as one example of an acceptable practice, however, neither state law nor the secretary of state require that any particular system of counting be used. Moderators should ensure that the system of counting they adopt is accurate and efficient." A link to this document could not be found on the internet, 15 July, 2012.

[20] See Endnote 17.

[21] Telephone conversation with Ernie Vose, July 2, 2008.

[22] See <http://car.elpasoco.com/NR/rdonlyres/60904F6C-F63B-48AC-93A4-DBC9356F6982/0/Final_Report_.pdf>, retrieved from the web, 30 June, 2008. (This link could not be found on the internet, 09 July, 2012.) A study called the Hand Counting Project was conducted by the Election Department of Colorado between January 6, 2008 and January 24, 2008, examining the read and tally & sort and stack methods. The study did not recommend either HCPB protocol—read and tally or sort and stack—but rather wanted readers to come to their own conclusions. Repeated phone calls and a requested e-mail were never answered by the Town Clerk who directed this study.

[23] Chain of custody of the ballots is very important in any HCPB method. However, should anything happen to the ballots themselves anywhere along the way, this written record would be an exact replication of the votes on the ballots themselves.

[24] The New Hampshire Election Procedure Manual 2006-2007 144, retrieved from the web January 4, 2008.

[25] See *"Chapter XII: On-Site Observations of the Hand-counting of Paper Ballots and Recommendations for the General Election Of 2008."* In the three read and tally elections I observed, I was able to see the names of the individuals or yes/no on the initiatives as the counters made their tallies.

[26] From Maine Revised Statutes Annotated (MRSA), *Conduct Of Elections'* Chapter 9, page 3, (Title 21-A §695). "The team counts each lot together; 1 member reads and the other member tallies. The team members then switch roles, so that the tally is done a second time. If they agree, that count is completed. If there is a discrepancy, the team must recount the race or races where the count was off...." The New Hampshire Election Procedure Manual 2006-2007 144, retrieved from the web January 4, 2008, which states that "…This process [sort and stack] enables team members to simultaneously examine each mark on each ballot at least once, and to keep things simple by identifying choice in a single race at a time. If one team member makes a mistake, the other can catch it…"

XIV

The Following are Some Necessary Elements of Observed, Secure Hand-Counted Paper Ballots (HCPB) Elections

The vote counting process must meet strict standards for transparency and accountability:

- Hand-counting is done for all races and initiatives, not only federal.
- The hand-counting process will be easily understood by a third grade student.
- No precinct is larger than 1000 registered voters.
- Hand-counting is done at each precinct, immediately after the polls close.
- Poll books of voters checking in and poll books of voters checking out must exactly match.
- Get rid of all e-poll books.
- The number of ballots counted must exactly match the number of ballots distributed.
- The number of ballots printed must match the number of ballots distributed, voted, and not voted.
- No absentee ballots will be allowed, except for people in dire need and these ballots must be accounted for, managed, and counted in a procedure that is yet to be written.
- Hand-counting is done by teams of opposing parties on the ballot, chosen by the parties themselves.
- Other smaller parties can also be on hand-counting teams, in addition to those opposing parties on the ballots—e.g., Greens.
- Hand-counting is done by new people coming in to count, not those who have been working at the polls all day.
- Hand-counters are paid a very good hourly rate. This not only pays

for one of the most important jobs in a democracy, but also keeps the money in the community and is far less expensive than buying, maintaining, upgrading and storing electronic voting machines.

- Hand-counting is done in full view of the public.
- Hand-counting is done twice and the results must match.
- Hand-counting is videotaped in real time by any member of the public who wants to do so, and also by official camera-people, one from all opposing parties on the ballot.
- All movements of ballots and ballot boxes are videotaped in real time by any member of the public who wants to do so, and also by official camerapeople, one from all opposing parties on the ballot.
- The entire hand-counting process is broadcast or streamed over the internet by election officials and by members of the public who wish to do so.
- Hand-counting results are posted at the precinct, in the windows, after the counting so that all can see easily after polls close.
- No electronic voting machines, computers, or modems of any kind are allowed in any part of the hand-count or the vote tabulation.
- The Vote-PAD provides a means for people with disabilities to mark a ballot without requiring the use of electronic voting machines. It is essential to the enfranchisement of people with disabilities, that they do not use electronic ballot marking devices (such as the AutoMARK) which are frequently marketed to assist people with disabilities. The AutoMark can steal votes just like any other electronic voting machine. In personal correspondence with Ellen Theisen, on May 1 and 2, 2011, Theisen said, "Vote-PAD is no longer available, except in the 22 Wisconsin municipalities that purchased it and are currently using it?. It provides the same paper ballot for people with disabilities as the ballot for others, and then all [ballots] are hand-counted together." See "Vote-PAD rocks the disabled vote."[1]
- The hand-count, which has been done twice, will be the official count of the election from each precinct.
- This section on chain of custody and security of the ballots and ballot boxes is a work in progress.
- The last two sections (Ballot and Ballot Box Transportation & Ballot Storage) of an article by Douglas W. Jones (University of Iowa Department of Computer Science) about Australian hand-counted paper ballot elections give many details of how to secure the ballots and their boxes.[2]

- See more details about security of ballots and their boxes in "*Chapter III: Hand-Counted Paper Ballots Now.*" Scroll down to the third paragraph from the end.

- Ballot boxes will be of clear plastic with a lock on each of the four corners. These boxes will be kept in full view of the election officials and the public at all times, from before the official opening time of the polls until the official election results are posted in the windows of each precinct.

- The locks on the ballot boxes will have two keys only, that is, one key will open two of the locks and another key will open the other two locks.

- There will be only one key for each of the two locks above. There will be no copies of keys.

- Election officials holding the keys must not be from the same political party.

- The ballot boxes will not be opened until all votes have been cast and the polls are closed.

- The ballot boxes will be opened in full view of the public.

- After the votes are hand-counted, the ballots will be placed in steel containers with seals on them.

- A secure chain of custody for the ballots and ballot boxes must be written from the precinct level to where they will be stored.

Furthermore, there are several problems with our voting process, not only that our votes are not counted as cast, because of the fraud and error associated with all electronic voting machines, but also, that even if these problems were all fixed, the electronic voting machines would continue to rig our elections. And even if we had secure hand-counted paper ballots (HCPB) elections, the problems listed below would still exist. Our voting system is a hydra-headed weapon of mass destruction:

- Suppression of the votes of students, low income people, African Americans, Latinas, elders.

- A whiteout of the news from any candidates the corporate media does not want to be elected.

- A whiteout of the news from the corporate media of any of the fraud and rigging that voting rights activists have been pointing out and writing about at least since Florida 2000 presidential race.

- Corrupt election officials who run our elections and have strong past and present ties to the right wing of the Republican Party.
- Corrupt and/or incompetent voting election officials from both Democratic and Republican parties, and most likely all the other parties too.
- Endless corporate money into coffers of candidates.
- Requiring of voter ID photos, which are issued only by the state, e.g., Department of Motor Vehicles, in order to vote.
- Absentee ballots, with both parties increasingly calling for more.
- Mail-in voting.
- The election of two senators from each state means, e.g., that the voters in North Dakota and Vermont have an influence that is hugely disproportionate to voters in California.
- Those conducting exit polls now adjust their exit polls to make them conform to the (corrupt) official counts, thus making the illusion of an honest election no matter how corrupt the election is.

This article originally appeared in Center for Hand-Counted Paper Ballots, 26 January, 2012 (http://www.handcountedpaperballots.org/documents/requirements.html).

Endnotes

[1] Kim Zetter, "Vote-PAD Rocks the Disabled Vote," Wired Magazine, 19 January, 2006 <http://www.wired.com/science/discoveries/news/2006/01/70036>.

[2] Douglas W. Jones,"Voting on Paper Ballots" specifically, see the sections "Ballot and Ballot Box Transportation" and "Ballot Storage" (the last two on the following link). The University Of Iowa Department of Computer Science, Voting and Elections web pages <http://www.cs.uiowa.edu/~jones/voting/paper.html>.

About the Author

SHEILA PARKS, ED.D., is a former college professor who left her career because she wanted to work to help make the world a better place and did not feel she was doing that in academia. Sheila works as intently on changing herself as she does on trying to change the outside world and views both the inner and outer as extremely important and inseparably entwined. She was in Occupy Boston and is the Founder of the Center for Hand-Counted Paper Ballots, http://www.handcountedpaperballots.org. Active in the current wave of voting rights since the crimes of the presidential election in Florida, 2000, she is against the use of all electronic voting machines in our elections and is for the solution of publicly observed, secure hand-counted paper ballots (HCPB) elections. An ardent and long time feminist, internationalist, and peace and justice activist, she defended the abortion clinics with her body for a very long time. She does not want to go back to doing that and fervently hopes that those of you who have not had to do so, never will.